Co-production

Public management research has in recent years paid increasing attention to the third sector, especially to its role in the provision of public services. Evidence of this is the rising number of publications on the topic, as well as a growing number of sessions and papers on the topic in academic conferences of the EGPA and IRSPM. However, much of the discussion on its role is motivated at least as much by ideology as by fact. We still lack a proper empirical understanding of what happens when the third sector is drawn into public service provision.

In this thematic presentation of Co-Production: The Third Sector and the Delivery of Public Services, we will try to enhance this understanding by presenting several new studies on the subject. We also introduce the concepts of co-production, co-management and co-governance as a conceptual framework that enables us to better understand such developments.

This book was previously published as a special issue of *Public Management Review*.

Victor Pestoff, Professor of Political Science, Mid-Sweden University, Östersund and also affiliated with Ersta Sköndal College, Stockholm, Sweden.

Taco Brandsen, Associate Professor at the Nijmegan School of Management, Nijmegan University, the Netherlands.

Co-production

The Third Sector and the Delivery of Public Services

Edited by
Victor Pestoff and Taco Brandsen

Routledge
Taylor & Francis Group
LONDON AND NEW YORK

First published 2008 by Routledge
4 Park Square, Milton Park, Abingdon, Oxon OX14 4RN
605 Third Avenue, New York, NY 10017

Routledge is an imprint of the Taylor & Francis Group, an informa business

Typeset in Perpetua by KnowledgeWorks Global Limited, Southampton, Hampshire, UK

British Library Cataloguing in Publication Data
A catalogue record for this book is available from the British Library

Library of Congress Cataloging in Publication Data

ISBN 13: 978-0-415-43963-3 (hbk)

CONTENTS

1. Co-production, The Third Sector and the Delivery of Public Services: An Introduction 1
Taco Brandsen and Victor Pestoff

2. Citizens and Co-Production of Welfare Services: Childcare in eight European countries 11
Victor Pestoff

3. Childcare, Co-Production and the Third Sector in Canada 29
Susan Prentice

4. Co-Management in Public Service Networks: The organizational effects 45
Taco Brandsen and Eelco van Hout

5. Co-Governance within Networks and the Non-Profit – For-Profit Divide: A cross-cultural perspective on the evolution of domiciliary elderly care 59
Ingo Bode

6. The Emergence of Local Non-Profit – Government Partnerships and the Role of Intermediary Organizations in Japan: Contractual relationships and the limits to co-governance 75
Ichiro Tsukamoto and Mariko Nishimura

7. Reflections on the Market, Networking and Trust 91
Isabel Vidal

8. Patterns of Co-Production in Public Services: Some concluding thoughts 99
Victor Pestoff, Stephen P. Osborne and Taco Brandsen

9. Notes on Contributors 105

Index 107

CO-PRODUCTION, THE THIRD SECTOR AND THE DELIVERY OF PUBLIC SERVICES

An introduction

Taco Brandsen and Victor Pestoff

INTRODUCTION

In recent years, public management research has paid increasing attention to the third sector, especially to its role in the provision of public services. Evidence of this is the rising number of publications on the topic, as well as a growing number of sessions and papers on the topic in conferences of the EGPA and IRSPM. However, many discussions on its role are motivated at least as much by ideology as by fact. We do not yet have a comprehensive empirical understanding of what happens when the third sector is drawn into public services. In this collection on *Co-Production: The Third Sector and the Delivery of Public Services*, we will try to enhance this understanding by presenting several new studies on the subject. In this introduction, we will propose a conceptual framework that enables us to understand better such developments.

The third sector comes under various other names, such as the voluntary sector, the (private) non-profit sector, the social economy, civil society, all with slightly different defining characteristics, and with a large degree of overlap. While it is important to be precise, the definitional issue can be crippling to the debate in third-sector research, so we will avoid it here. When we refer to the third sector, we include all those groups and organizations grouped under other labels, accepting that it is a 'loose and baggy monster' (Kendall and Knapp 1995) without trying to cage it in.

One reason for the growing interest in the third sector is its involvement in the provision of public services. In some countries, the third sector has traditionally played a large role as in Germany and the Netherlands, where it has been an essential part of the construction of the post-war welfare state. In others, like the UK, it took shape in the context of outsourcing in the 1990s and in New Public Management. In addition, there has been the growth of organized initiatives in which citizens play a direct role in the production of the service, so far largely ignored in public management literature. This encourages researchers to examine the real benefits of involving this type of actor.

Another reason for the surge of interest in the third sector is, paradoxically, that it has been losing some of its distinctiveness. As a result of contracting out, privatization and performance measurement, the traditional boundaries between market, state and third sector have been breaking down, leading to the emergence of a class of organizational hybrids (Evers and Laville 2004; Brandsen *et al.* 2005). In concrete terms, it means that the third-sector organizations have taken on more characteristics of state organizations (e.g. in terms of formalization) and of market organizations (e.g. maximizing their income, but without maximizing their profit). Although no organization can be regarded as 'pure', many organizations now reach the point where the ideal types of state, market or third sector no longer help us truly to understand them.

One reaction to such developments has been isolationism: the call for a strict demarcation of the sector, both in a conceptual and a normative sense. For instance, it leads to pleas for third-sector organizations to avoid close association with the state. However, for better or worse, a significant part of the third sector has opted for closer integration with states and markets. In some countries, this dates back to the nineteenth century (e.g. in Germany and the Netherlands), or the early twentieth century (as in Sweden), while it came later in others (e.g. the UK in the 1990s). This has undeniably changed them, leading some to claim that they have changed to the point where they have lost their distinctiveness from state organizations. It is even conceivable, although this perspective needs to be further developed, that the third sector can be better understood in terms of certain aspects of public services, rather than as a distinct cluster of organizations (cf. Evers 2005). Such aspects can be adopted by organizations that we would not normally regard as third sector. Dekker (2001) has mentioned the example of public schools in The Netherlands that copied participative structures from religious schools and benefited as a result. Likewise, it has been argued that non-profit social housing providers can dampen overall rent levels, by competing with commercial providers, and 'civilize' the housing market (Kemeny 1995).

Here the issue takes on a wider relevance. Policymakers are not primarily interested in the third sector *per se*, but in what it can contribute to the quality of public services. Research can help to determine the exact benefits of its involvement. More precisely, this concerns the relationships between two variables: the role of the third sector in public service provision and the manner in which such services are produced. Please note our use of the plural 'relationships', for, as we will argue the connection is a far more dynamic one than is often supposed. The concept of co-production potentially offers a means of capturing a significant part of the quality of this dynamic.

THE BACKGROUND OF THE CO-PRODUCTION CONCEPT

Originally, the concept of co-production related primarily to the involvement of citizens or clients in production, i.e. direct user involvement, either in the public or private sectors. It generated great interest among public administration scholars in America in the 1970s and the 1980s (see Parks *et al.* 1999 [1981] for a good overview), and was originally developed by the Workshop in Political Theory and Policy Analysis at Indiana University. During the 1970s they struggled with the dominant theories of urban governance underlying policy recommendations of massive centralization. Scholars and public officials argued that citizens as clients would receive more effective and efficient services delivered by professional staff employed in a large bureaucratic agency. After studying police services in several metropolitan areas, however, they had not found a single instance where a large centralized police department was able to provide better direct service, more equitably delivered or at a lower cost to neighbourhoods located in surrounding jurisdictions (Ostrom 1999).

Thus, they stumbled on several myths of public production. One was the notion of a single producer being responsible for urban services within each jurisdiction. In fact, they normally found several agencies, as well as private firms, producing immediate response services (a finding that supports the network approach increasingly current in public management research). More important, they also realized that the production of a service, as contrasted to a good, was difficult without the active participation of those supposedly receiving the service. Thus, they developed the term *co-production* to describe the potential relationship that could exist between the 'regular' producer (street-level police officers, schoolteachers or health workers) and 'clients' who want to be transformed by the service into safer, better-educated or healthier persons. Co-production was one way through which synergy could occur between what a government does and what citizens do (Ostrom 1999). This use of the term 'co-production' had a clear micro focus on the role of individuals or groups in the production of such services, although their involvement could have clear ramifications for both the meso and macro levels of society.

In the UK, co-production has been used more recently to analyse the role of voluntary and community organizations (VCOs) in the provision of public services (Osborne and McLaughlin 2004). Here the term 'co-production' appears to imply a more restricted service delivery role for VCOs in the provision of community services, i.e. that of a service agent or provider. Other terms, such as 'co-management' or 'co-ordination', refer to a broader role for VCOs in local service management. Co-governance, on the other hand, refers to the role of VCOs in policy formulation and community governance, as illustrated by the Voluntary Sector Compact(s) at both the national and local levels. Here we find Local Strategic Partnerships in area regeneration (Osborne and McLaughlin 2004), but there is a notable absence of corporatist structures here. The term 'co-production' has also recently been introduced in a continental European context to refer to the growing organized involvement of citizens in the production of their own welfare services (Pestoff 2004; Vamstad 2004). The latter adheres more to the US than to UK usage of the term co-production, where parent participation in parent co-operative childcare provides the main empirical reference (Pestoff 1998).

Despite the differences in emphasis, what all these studies share is the notion that the involvement of the third sector (whether as groups of citizens or organizations) transforms the delivery of public services. What they also indicate is that the nature of the relationship between the third sector and the production process is a dynamic one. The involvement of citizens transforms the service, but they are themselves transformed by the service. Likewise, the involvement of the third sector allows it to deliver services differently, but in doing so it is itself incorporated into the institutionalized system of provision. Some aspects or components of the system rub off on one another through the production process. This means we must go beyond the perspective of a one-way relationship between state and third sector as principal and agent, or provider and recipient. The concept of co-production emphasizes the shared character of the production process.

What we attempt in the next section is to draw together different elements of past literature and integrate them into a coherent conceptual framework. This framework will link the other contributions to this collection.

DIFFERENT MODES OF CO-OPERATION

On the basis of a typology developed by Osborne and McLaughlin (2004) we will break down the original co-production concepts into three potential manifestations: co-production, co-management and co-governance. All refer to a type of co-operation in which the third sector has a direct influence on the nature of the service (i.e. output). Strictly speaking these concepts are not exclusively linked to certain levels of analysis (micro – meso – macro), although there may be an empirical correspondence. For instance, co-management tends to be most relevant to the meso level. However, the concepts refer primarily to different types of co-operation.

- *Co-governance* refers to an arrangement, in which the third sector participates in the planning and delivery of public services.
- *Co-management* refers to an arrangement, in which third-sector organizations produce services in collaboration with the state.
- *Co-production*, in the restricted use of the term, refers to an arrangement where citizens produce their own services at least in part. This is a specific interpretation of user involvement, although there are of course various other types (cf. Evers 2006).

Each of these links to broader strands of literature, some of which will be discussed in the other contributions. We distinguish the three concepts along two dimensions:

(1) A distinction between the organizational and the individual level. Whereas co-management refers primarily to interactions between organizations, co-production refers to voluntary efforts by individual citizens.

(2) A distinction between phases in the policy cycle, between planning and production. This separates co-governance from the other two concepts: the former focuses on policy formulation, the latter on implementation.

That means that the concepts are not mutually exclusive. It is possible that third-sector organizations delivering public services have participatory structures, so that co-management and co-production are combined. Alternatively, production is organized solely around the users of services, in which case there is only co-production.

We have chosen to bring together all contributions to this collection under the joint heading of 'co-production'. We are aware that this may give rise to some initial confusion, when the term also refers to the more restricted meaning of user involvement. However, it does seem to be the right label for what we are describing, as well as a mark of our indebtedness to the user involvement debate. Therefore we have chosen to ignore the inconvenience of double usage.

CONTENTS

This collection on *Co-Production: The Third Sector and Delivery of Public Services* will examine how third-sector involvement has changed the delivery of public services, and how this in turn has changed the third sector. Each contribution has a different angle on this theme, and integrates the concepts with existing strands of theory.

Victor Pestoff's contribution on 'Citizens and Co-Production of Welfare Services: Childcare in Eight European Countries' addresses the issue of what role the state, market and third sector should play in the provision of welfare services. A growing number of scholars question the viability of liberal representative democracy and the welfare state in an 'Age of Organizations', dominated by the big organizations found in both the public and private sector. They argue that the state is overextended and democracy is stretched to its limits. Walzer proposes to socialize the means of distributing welfare services through greater involvement of the recipients of such services, and Hirst calls for devolving as many of the functions of the state as possible to civil society, while retaining public funding. But, how and where do citizens come into the picture? Missing from these macro proposals is the micro perspective of the role of citizens provided by the concept co-production.

This contribution starts out by describing the concept of co-production, as found in public administration literature. The focus here is on greater citizen participation in the provision of public services. The literature review demonstrates several advantages of co-production, but also some major hurdles to be overcome. The second part ties the concept of co-production to a discussion of parents' participation in the provision of childcare services in Europe. Finally, the importance of co-production for promoting the development and renewal of democracy and the welfare state is discussed. It also calls attention to differences between co-production, co-management and co-governance in terms of citizen participation.

Susan Prentice's contribution on 'Childcare, Co-Production and the Third Sector in Canada' provides a timely review of developments in Canadian childcare, in particular the role of the third sector, as a major provider of such services. The author focuses mostly on the role of parent-users and the third sector as co-producers of childcare services, and documents differences between the provinces in providing such services. The third sector is quite dominant in this sector, due to the virtual absence of publicly provided services. However, Prentice observes that the third sector's role is limited to co-production and that there is little room for either co-management or co-governance. Typical of Canadian childcare are a 'frustrated national and provincial policy capacity, a high degree of commercial childcare, inequities in service distribution, and the burdening of parent-users (particularly mothers)'. This infrastructure makes a national system of early learning and childcare 'structurally unobtainable'.

Taco Brandsen and Eelco van Hout's 'Co-management in Public Service Networks: The Organizational Effects' deals with the issue of how third-sector organizations are changed through their association with the state in the context of public service provision. There is a tendency in research on this topic to place the third sector in the role of the victim, emphasizing processes of rationalization and the loss of distinctiveness. While this is certainly significant, it underplays the role of such organizations as active agents of change. To understand this, it is crucial to analyse the processes occurring within the organizations. They must be able to cope with tensions that to some extent confront all providers of public services. The production of services often requires both competition and co-operation with network partners. Expanding requirements for accountability reduce the scope for balancing multiple organizational objectives. The supply of public services is fragmented and demand tends to be unitary, encouraging suppliers to diversify.

Consequently, the organizations are faced with simultaneous pressures for differentiation and integration. Empirical research shows several means by which they alleviate these pressures: acquiring soft skills, moving from staffing to sourcing, strengthening informal mechanisms of co-ordination and changing management style. In such a way, they adapt to the network context in which they operate, and as a result, they contribute actively to network integration and to innovation in the public services.

Ingo Bode's 'Co-governance within Networks and the nonprofit – forprofit divide: A cross-cultural perspective on the evolution of domiciliary elderly care' provides a good comparative overview of contemporary developments in the field of elder care in three European countries: England, France and Germany. In each of these countries, some form of co-governance existed prior to the more recent advent of quasi-market type of system. In social care, as in other areas of the welfare state, there existed corporatist structures that maintained a 'domain consensus' between welfare bureaucrats, professionals and the third-sector providers of domiciliary services to the elder. In France, there was a clearer separation between state and third sector, but nevertheless patterns of 'local corporatism' developed, 'symbiotic relationships between public and voluntary agencies based on agreements between notables and local politicians'. In England, the public and voluntary sectors were only weakly coupled, although consensual co-operation took root in some places.

In all countries, the establishment of quasi-market systems has weakened previously existing systems of governance. Within the new arrangements, the third sector's contribution to service provision shifts towards co-management. Co-governance has become more indirect, even in Germany where the associational pillars still offer a good infrastructure for interorganizational co-ordination. However, the third sector's role as campaign organizations and as a lobby for the elderly and better quality care provision still remains notable in all cases.

Ichiro Tsukamoto and Mariko Nishimura focus on 'The Emergence of Local Nonprofit – Government Partnerships and the Role of Intermediary Organizations in Japan: Contractual Relationships and the Limits to Co-Governance'. In recent years, the Japanese third sector has been increasingly involved in government-funded service delivery, spurring the growth of co-management. However, the contractual relationships between third-sector organizations and governments have caused a loss of distinctiveness and independence. Co-governance is weakly developed. Generally, the third sector has been ineffective at creating voluntary and horizontal networks beyond individual organizations. The authors therefore advocate an increased and more independent role for intermediary organizations. They regard three issues as crucial in this respect: (1) the development of a mixed resource strategy; (2) the establishment of representative and networking structures; (3) stronger political functions such as advocacy and the mobilization of collective influence on government policy.

Isabel Vidal's 'Reflection on the Market, Networking and Trust' provides us with an economic perspective of the why and how of the different forms of governance, management and production of certain public services. From the theoretical approach of *why* the supposition is made that the terms of co-governance, co-management and co-production are associated with the concepts of a division of labour, specialization, networking and collaboration among different players pursuing different goals. The theory of networks and the concept of trust are necessary to explain the *how*. For an organization taking part in the network, it means that its network partners and other organizations value the organization positively and think that it does things properly. The expected objective of this co-operation is a better adaption to the preferences of different groups at any given moment.

On the basis of the contributions in this collection, Victor Pestoff, Stephen Osborne and Taco Brandsen reconsider the concept of co-production and discuss issues that might be of interest to the future research agenda. Specifically, they mention the relationships between different roles of the third sector, links with the analysis of welfare state reform and the function of co-production.

REFERENCES

Brandsen, T., van de Donk, W. and Putters, K. (2005) Griffins or Chameleons? Hybridity as a Permanent and Inevitable Characteristic of the Third Sector, *International Journal of Public Administration*. 28: 9–10 pp749–65.

Dekker, P. (2001) 'What Crisis, What Challenges? When Nonprofitness Makes no Difference' in H. K. Anheier and J. Kendall (eds) *Third Sector Policy At The Crossroads*. London: Routledge, pp61–68.

Evers, A. (2005) Mixed Welfare Systems and Hybrid Organizations: Changes in the Governance and Provision of Social Services, *International Journal of Public Administration*. 28: 9–10 pp737–48.

—— (2006) 'Complementary and Conflicting: The Different Meanings of "User Involvement" in Social Services' in A. L. Matthies (ed.) *Nordic Civic Society Organisations and The Future of Welfare Services: A Model for Europe?* Copenhagen: Nordic Council.

Evers, A. and Laville, J.-L. (2004) 'Social Services by Social Enterprises: On the Possible Contributions of Hybrid Organizations and a Civil Society' in A. Evers and J.-L. Laville (eds) *The Third Sector in Europe*. Cheltenham: Edward Elgar.

Kemeny, J. (1995) *From Public Housing to the Social Market: Rental Policy Strategies in Comparative Perspective*, London: Routledge.

Kendall, J. and Knapp, M. (1995) 'A Loose and Baggy Monster: Boundaries, Definitions and Typologies' in J. D. Smith, C. Rochester and R. Hedley (eds) *An Introduction to the Voluntary Sector*. London: Routledge.

Osborne, S. and McLaughlin, K. (2004) The Cross-Cutting Review of the Voluntary Sector: Where Next for Local Government Voluntary Sector Relationships?, *Regional Studies*. 38: 5 pp573 – 82.

Ostrom, E. (1999) 'Crossing the Great Divide: Coproduction, Synergy, and Development' in M. McGinnis (ed.) *Polycentric Governance and Development: Readings from the Workshop in Political Theory and Policy Analysis*. Ann Arbor, MI: University of Michigan Press.

Parks, R. B., Baker, P. C., Kiser, L., Oakerson, R., Ostrom, E., Ostrom, V., Percy, S. L., Vandivort, M. B., Whitaker, G. P. and Wison, R. (1981) Consumers as Co-Producers of Public Services: Some Economic and Institutional Considerations, *Policy Studies Journal*. 9: 7 pp1001 – 11. Reprinted in McGinnis, M. ed. (1999) *Local Public Economies: Readings from the Workshop in Political Theory and Policy Analysis*. Ann Arbor, MI: University of Michigan Press.

Pestoff, V. (1998) *Beyond the Market and State: Social Enterprises and Civil Democracy in a Welfare Society*, Aldershot, Brookfield, NJ, Singapore & Sidney: Ashgate.

—— (2004) Co-Production and Personal Social Services: Childcare in Eight European Countries. Paper presented at EGPA conference, September, Ljubljana, Slovenia.

Vamstad, J. (2004) Co-Production as a Defining Principle – a New Typology for Provision of Welfare Services in Sweden. Paper presented at EGPA conference, September, Ljubljana, Slovenia.

CITIZENS AND CO-PRODUCTION OF WELFARE SERVICES

Childcare in eight European countries

Victor Pestoff

INTRODUCTION

What role should the state and market play in the provision of welfare services? Should the state provide most welfare services, as today in universal or Social Democratic welfare states in Scandinavia, or should services be privatized and provided by the market, as proposed by neo-liberals? This is a hotly debated issue in all European countries and one of the main, if not the main question posed to the voters in all European elections in the last twenty to twenty-five years. As hotly debated as it is, it fails to consider the potential role of civil society, or the third sector and citizens. What role should the third sector play in providing welfare services, and what role should citizens have in producing such services? Answers to the latter question reflect different perspectives on citizens and different views of citizenship. Are citizens merely passive consumers of welfare services that are provided either by the state or market, or can they play an active role in producing some kinds of welfare services? Is citizenship restricted to voting in general elections, consuming goods and services, paying taxes and abiding by the laws of the land, or does it imply both rights and responsibilities that go beyond this limited view of citizenship?

Co-production or citizen involvement in the provision of public services generated a flurry of interest among public administration scholars in America in the 1970s and the 1980s (see Parks *et al.* 1999 [1981] for a good overview). The concept of co-production could prove highly relevant to proposals for democratic and welfare state reforms. Co-production provides a missing piece of the puzzle for reforming democracy and the welfare state. It contributes a view and understanding of conditions at the micro level or the site of production of welfare services. This perspective is often missing in many of the more macro-oriented perspectives found in the following.

More than twenty years ago Barber (1984) compared thin democracy to strong democracy and proposed a more active role for citizens. Walzer (1988) argued for 'more participative and decentralized forms for service provision' (p. 21) – that make room for self-help and local initiative. He contrasted earlier calls to nationalize the means of production of goods with today's need to socialize the means of distribution of welfare services. This needed to be actively supported by a state-sponsored socialization, i.e. the democratic transformation of state agencies at the local level or the transfer of authority and resources to voluntary organizations (1988: 21). Most important was to increase the number of distributors who are also recipients or potential recipients of welfare services. Only then would they have a greater say in welfare management. He argued that greater recipient involvement can be worked out within a democratized system of state supervision or through the activities of voluntary organizations (1988: 22).

He proposed several ways of recruiting more distributors of welfare services, including paying a nominal wage to volunteers and instituting a new national service for providing welfare services (1988: 22). In post-industrial societies a growing number of civil servants work in welfare services. But, they do not have a natural monopoly on helping, even if they are professional helpers. The welfare state co-exists with a welfare society, even if the latter is relatively weak today and requires the continued and sustained support of the former (1988: 25). Walzer noted that his suggestion requires a major reform of local democracy and also an effort to extend the reach of voluntary organizations. At the same time the state needs to be strong enough to superintend and subsidize the work of citizens and volunteers. A lively and supportive welfare society framed, but not controlled, by a strong welfare state would represent a fundamental transformation in the relations of distribution or service provision (1988: 26) and also a reform of the relations between 'the rulers and the ruled'.

Hirst (1994) argued that liberal representative democracy is over extended today. Democracy is stretched to its limits, due to the growth of the modern welfare state, and cannot function as intended – to control the public administration. Associative democracy calls for a much more active role for the third sector and citizens in providing goods and services, in order to return democracy to what it once was – the will of the people. He suggested that many major policy networks be extended to include all the governed. Associative democracy means devolving as many of the functions of the state as possible to civil society, while retaining public funding, and democratizing as many as possible of the organizations of civil society (1994). This should not simply be seen as nostalgia for returning to a lost 'golden age', but rather as a way of developing and renewing democracy, as well as a means for curbing the growth and dominance of big organizations, both in business and government.

In a lucid analysis of power Galbraith (1984, 1986) spoke of the 'Age of Organizations'. Conditional power gains its influence by persuasion and changing beliefs. It stems from organizations, mostly big organizations regardless of sector, i.e. public or private. More recently in a discussion of 'democracy and governance', Hirst (2002) contrasts an 'organizational society', with its large public and private bureaucracies to the normally smaller organizations found in civil society. He called for large-scale institutional reform of both state and social institutions. The aim of these reforms is to restore limited government by involving civil society in the functions of the state and to transform the organizations of the latter from top – down bureaucracies into constitutionally ordered democratically self-governing associations (2002: 28). However, associative self-government would supplement and extend representative government, not replace it. Democracy at the national level would be strengthened and made more viable by democratizing civil society. Governments' principal task would, therefore, be to raise and distribute revenue to associations and the provision of a constitutional ordering and supervision of the institutions of civil society (2002: 30).

What does greater citizen participation in the provision of welfare services, or co-production, imply for the development and renewal of democracy today? In what ways can and do citizens participate in the provision of public services? How do differences in citizen participation relate to the development and renewal of democracy? Co-production will first be considered from a theoretical perspective and then illustrated by the involvement of parents in childcare services in Europe. Materials for this study come from the TSFEPS Project, Changing Family Structures and Social Policy: Childcare Services as Sources of Social Cohesion, a comparative European study between 2002 and 2005 of childcare services in eight European nations.[1] They are Belgium, Bulgaria, England, France, Germany, Italy, Spain and Sweden. Thus, the study merges two strands of thought or two types of questions concerning citizen participation. First it addresses the theoretical literature on co-production of public services. Second, it explores citizen participation in childcare services in eight European countries. Finally, it reaches some conclusions about the role of co-production in developing and renewing democracy and the welfare state.

CO-PRODUCTION

There are numerous important issues for understanding citizen involvement in the production of public services. A review of the literature provides a good starting point for identifying some of the most relevant issues. Co-production differs notably from the traditional model of public service production in which public officials are exclusively charged with responsibility for designing and providing services to citizens, who in turn only demand, consume and evaluate them. The dominant model of public service production, according to Sharp (1980), is based on two distinct spheres: one of regular (public) producers and a second sphere of goods and service-consuming clients or citizens, interest groups, etc. Feedback between these spheres can be problematic. By contrast, the co-production model is based on the assumption of an active, participative populace of consumer producers. When the two spheres overlap to a greater or lesser degree the feedback between them becomes an internal process. Service delivery is a joint venture involving both citizens and government agents (Whitaker 1980). Thus, co-production implies citizen participation in the execution or implementation of public policies.

Co-production is, therefore, noted by the mix of activities that both public service agents and citizens contribute to the provision of public services. The former are involved as professionals or 'regular producers', while 'citizen production' is based on voluntary efforts of individuals or groups to enhance the quality and/or quantity of services they receive (Brudney and England 1983; Ostrom 1999; Parks *et al.* 1999 [1981]). In complex societies there is a division of labour and most persons are engaged in full-time production of goods and services as regular producers. However, individual consumers or groups of consumers may also contribute to the production of goods and services, as consumer producers. This mixing may occur directly or indirectly.

If co-production occurs, it takes place as a result of technological, economic and institutional or political influences (Parks *et al.* 1999 [1981]). Technology determines whether there are production functions for a service where both regular and consumer producer activities contribute to the output. Economic considerations determine whether it is efficient to mix regular and consumer producer activities to produce the service. Institutional considerations determine whether appropriate mixing is permitted in situations where co-production is technically feasible and economically efficient, and whether mixing is discouraged where it is inefficient (Parks *et al.* 1981: 1002).

Technical relationships among regular and consumer producers are crucial and can either result in a situation where their inputs are substitutes for each other, or they are interdependent of each other. An economic mix depends on the substitutability or interdependence of producing a particular service and the relative wages and opportunity costs for regular and consumer producers. If it is a case of interdependence there are likely to be both regular and consumer production inputs. Neither the regular nor consumer producers can supply the service alone: inputs from both are necessary. Still institutional incentives are necessary for co-production to exist (Parks *et al.* 1981: 1002 – 6).

Percy (1984) notes that co-production occurs when *both* consumers and regular producers undertake efforts to produce the *same* goods or services. There is no requirement that their efforts be taken through direct interactions, but only that they be undertaken more or less simultaneously. In addition, Rich (1981) identifies other vital dimensions of co-production. He distinguishes between positive and negative, co-operative and compliant, active and passive as well as individual and collective co-production. Co-production does not require the formal organization of citizens, but organizations are also a critical variable, since they can enhance the levels of co-production and may facilitate the co-ordination between citizens and public agencies (Rich 1981).

However, Warren *et al.* (1982) and Rosentraub and Warren (1987), warned against too broad a definition. They argued that by narrowing the concept one also excludes civic activities normally associated with citizenship, termed ancillary or auxiliary production, and actions taken totally separately from regular service agents, known as parallel production. Ancillary actions are expected forms of behaviour for citizens, such as obeying the law and following regulations or reporting crime. Parallel production involves services similar to those provided by public agencies, but produced by individuals without contact or co-operation with public agencies.

Co-production is often seen as an approach to the enhancement of municipal productivity. Warren *et al.* (1982) maintain that co-production can lead to cost reductions, higher service quality and expanded opportunities for citizens to participate in decisions concerning public services. The latter can result in greater satisfaction with and support for public services. Thus, co-production becomes an important means of enhancing both the quality and quantity of public services. However, savings to the public budget from co-production are constrained by the amount of substitution that can effectively be undertaken between citizens and service agents or public employees (Brudney 1984). Citizens normally lack the training and experience to perform services requiring specialized training. Moreover, substituting paid personnel with voluntary efforts means that some of the costs are transferred to the co-producers themselves. The costs are not eliminated, merely shifted to the citizens.

Percy (1984) maintained that the scope of the benefits resulting from co-productive efforts may affect a citizen's decision about the types and frequency of co-production undertaken. Where the benefits of the citizens' efforts go primarily to the citizen-producers themselves, co-production is likely to be greatest. There is a direct correspondence between resources committed and benefits received. However, where the benefits are more broadly scattered among the population in general, citizens' co-productive actions are less frequent (Percy 1984). Here there is a 'free-rider' problem that needs to be identified and analysed.

Rich (1981) notes that citizens may consider the net benefits of their voluntary efforts in terms of fellowship, self-esteem or other intangible benefits stemming from them. He emphasized the interface between the government and voluntary sectors and noted the importance of recognizing that voluntary action always takes place in a political context. The individual cost/benefit analysis and the decision to co-operate with voluntary efforts, as well as the effectiveness of these efforts, can be conditioned by the structure of political institutions. Centralized service delivery tends to make articulation of demands more costly for citizens and to inhibit governmental responsiveness, while citizen participation seems to fare better in decentralized service delivery (Ostrom 1975).

Moreover, Percy (1984) also stated that organizational arrangements could facilitate or hinder co-production. In particular, resistance to co-production strategies may be encountered in public service agencies. Service workers and public administrators may see themselves as trained workers and therefore resent or resist the intrusion of untrained and inexperienced workers. Without the tacit support of public employees, the involvement of citizens in production activities might create more problems than it solves (Rosentraub and Warren 1987). Typical examples of co-production found in the early literature on the USA include public safety and security, education, fire protection, recreation and even solid waste collection and disposal (Percy 1984).

While co-production initially attracted a lot of attention in the USA in the 1970s and 1980s, since then involving people and groups outside the Government in producing public services has received more sporadic interest. Ostrom (1999) analysed co-production in developing countries. Here she focused on suburban water supply in Brazil and primary education in Nigeria. According to her all public goods and services are potentially produced by the regular producer and by those who are frequently referred to as the client. However, the term client is a passive term; indicating that they are acted upon. Co-production, by contrast, implies that citizens can play an active role in producing public goods and services of consequence to them (Ostrom 1999: 347).

She points out that, on the one hand, no market can survive without extensive public goods provided by governmental agencies, but, on the other hand, that no government can be efficient and equitable without considerable input from citizens. 'Co-production of many goods and services, normally considered to be public goods by government agencies and [by] citizens organized into polycentric systems, is crucial for achieving higher levels of welfare in developing countries, particularly those that are poor' (1999:

347). Her perspective could, of course, be extended to cover welfare services in many developed countries. Co-production is also essential for sustaining current levels of welfare service provision in European welfare systems facing sharp budget constraints, the crunch of globalization and losing jobs to low wage countries.

Renewed academic interest in co-production recognizes that in many important areas of government activity it is impossible to deliver services without the contributions of time and effort by clients. Today there is a growing interest in understanding co-production or greater citizen participation in the production of public services. Alford (2002) distinguished between three sources of motivation for citizen participation in public-sector services: material, solidarity and expressive incentives. He examined four cases of participation in public-sector services in Australia ranging from simple to complex: the use of post codes in postal services, participation by long-term unemployed in training programmes, maintenance activities by tenants in public high-rise housing complexes and taxpayer collaboration with income tax requirements (Alford 2002).

He noted that government reformers often urge the adoption of a private-sector-style 'customer focus', but critics see it as inappropriate, in particular because it diminishes citizenship. He argued that interactions between most public-sector organizations and their clients differ in several fundamental ways from the private-sector customer transactions. From a social exchange perspective government organizations need some things from service recipients – such as their co-operation and compliance – which are essential for effective organizational performance. Eliciting those things requires not only meeting the material needs of citizens, but also their symbolic or normative expectations. Thus, involving citizen co-production is consistent with an active model of citizenship (Alford 2002).

In addition to the basic exchange where services are exchanged for money, there is also an exchange of the client's time and efforts for heightening the value the client perceives in certain situations. However, material rewards and sanctions are ineffective in eliciting the requisite client contributions of time and effort in all but the most simple of tasks. Rather, many clients are motivated by more complex non-material incentives, such as intrinsic rewards or social, solidarity and expressive values. These different motivators elicit co-production in different contextual circumstances. The more public the value consumed by clients, the more complex the motivations for them to co-produce. He concludes that 'eliciting co-production is a matter of heightening the value that clients receive from the services by making more explicit its nonmaterial aspects through intrinsic rewards, solidarity incentives or normative appeal' (Alford 2002: 48).

In Scandinavia the idea of enhancing the role of citizens in providing welfare services seldom gains attention from scholars and politicians. However, citizens currently contribute much of their time and effort to the production of welfare services, both as parents in relation to childcare or youth sports activities and sports clubs, as well as relatives in terms of eldercare. Thus, they directly contribute to the realization of the final value of good quality childcare, healthful youth sports activities and/or good quality eldercare, although such services are primarily financed by taxes. A recent report to the Swedish parliamentary committee, *Ansvarskommittén*, calls for a greater role for citizen participation and direct democracy in continued reforms of the Swedish welfare state (Häggroth 2005). In order to come to grips with the growing democracy deficit and to renew the legitimacy of the welfare state, citizens should play a greater role in the delivery of welfare services the report concludes.

In a Scandinavian context important public services where co-production might be promoted include welfare services, like childcare, elementary and higher education, health care, eldercare, handicap care, leisure activities, etc. In a universal, tax-financed welfare state like that found in the Scandinavian countries the consumer is a citizen, while the buyer or purchaser of services may be a public body, unless vouchers are used, and finally the provider of such services is often a municipal or private body. Although the services can be financed by taxes, fees or both, they may also require that the consumer of the services contribute some of his/her time to realize the full value of the service. Many welfare services also build on enduring relations between the consumer and providers of such services rather than on one-time relations of an *ad hoc* nature. Pestoff (1999 [1998]) explores both parent and staff participation in parent co-ops, worker co-ops and voluntary organizations providing childcare services for pre-school children in Sweden and contrasts them with the services provided by the public sector (Pestoff 1999 [1998]).

He shows that the motives of parents for choosing one type of childcare facility or another express the values they hope to promote by becoming co-producers. Their motives can either be instrumental or expressive, but most parents combine both, similar to the pattern found by Alford (2002). Co-production and the work obligation associated with many alternative providers of pre-school services in Sweden help to eliminate uncertainty in the relationship between producers and consumers of these services. It provides parents with greater insights into the quality of the services and gives them influence on decisions of how to run the childcare facility. Moreover, the provision of welfare services through social enterprises that facilitate co-production alters the relationship between the state and citizens in a fundamental way. Citizens are no longer passive consumers of public services who are defined mainly by their roles as tax payers and voters who exercise their political rights every second, third, fourth or fifth year. Rather they become active participants in the production of important welfare services they demand themselves (Alford 2002).

Peters (1996 [1994]) discussed four emerging models of public-sector provision of goods and services. He regards the participatory model as an alternative to both the old bureaucratic one and to New Public Management. A participatory state depends upon both its citizens and front-line staff becoming involved in making some choices about policy and social services. Similar to the market model, a participatory model would also give citizens more choice and direct control over the providers of various goods and services. But the manner in which these choices would be exercised in a participatory state would be much more overtly political. Rather than voting with their feet, through vouchers or their Euros, dollars, crowns or yen, citizens would vote through some sort of political process. They might participate in referenda of local policy or in local representative structures, like parent involvement in school committees (Peters 1996 [1994]: 15). Alternatively, participation can take place in non-representative, but nevertheless democratic structures for providing welfare services, like co-operative childcare in Sweden (Pestoff 1999 [1998]). The important point however is that citizens become involved in the co-production of the services that they both need and demand.

Co-production will be illustrated by parents' participation in childcare services. Materials for this study come from the TSFEPS Project, Changing Family Structures and Social Policy: Childcare Services as Sources of Social Cohesion, a comparative European study between 2002 and 2005 of childcare services in eight European nations. They are Belgium, Bulgaria, England, France, Germany, Italy, Spain and Sweden. Case studies of different providers of childcare in two cities[2] per country contributed the empirical materials for the discussion of parent participation in childcare.

PARTICIPATION IN CHILDCARE SERVICES IN EIGHT EUROPEAN COUNTRIES

Participation in childcare services takes different forms in different countries in the TSFEPS Project. It ranges from high to low and can be found at different levels of analysis, both at the aggregate or city-wide level and at the individual childcare centre. Participation involves different dimensions or aspects, such as economic, political, pedagogical and social participation. It also involves different groups or stakeholders, like the parents, staff and public authorities responsible for providing and funding pre-school services, and in some cases third-sector organizations, TSOs, and even a few for-profit firms that provide such services. We begin our discussion with economic participation, then consider political, pedagogic and finally social participation by parents.

Economic participation in childcare services can either involve the contribution of money, in-kind donations or time by parents. Parent fees are found in most countries and they represent one kind of economic participation. However, they are normally limited by law to a certain proportion of the total costs for providing such services, and not set by market circumstances related to supply and demand. Parents normally do not gain additional benefits from greater economic participation. But, parents are also expected to make contributions in-kind for the running of childcare services in some countries. This is particularly striking in the former socialist countries where the state or local authorities often lack the funds necessary to maintain reasonable material standards in childcare facilities. Here parents feel obliged to contribute both their time and various material things necessary for keeping the services running, in addition to regular parent fees. But some type of economic contribution in-kind can also be found to a lesser degree in countries with less developed systems of childcare provision and in services arranged or initiated by parents themselves.

By contrast, contributions of time in most EU countries are normally associated with parental participation in the running and management of childcare facilities, like those found in France, Germany and Sweden (Evers and Riedel 2003; Fraisse and Bucolo 2003; Strandbrink and Pestoff 2003). In parent co-operative or parent initiative services there is often a work obligation, which excludes many parents who do not have flexible working conditions that permit them to make such contributions in time. In particular, single parent families find it difficult to meet the extra time demands of such services in most facilities included here (Evers and Riedel 2003; Fraisse and Bucolo 2003; Strandbrink and Pestoff 2003).

Political participation by parents can either take indirect, representative or corporatist forms in sector-wide municipal decision-making bodies or it can involve direct parental participation in decision-making bodies at the level of individual childcare centres or site of service production. Small parent-run and managed childcare services often depend on the efforts of all the parents, not only a few elected representatives. Participation can also take the form of elected parental representation in the consultative committees found in public services in many countries, often stipulated by law. However, they tend to be restricted to consultations with parents rather than to involve them in decision making.

Pedagogical participation by parents is both a natural and highly disputed phenomenon at the same time. Parents and the home are a natural part of children's growth and development and this argues for involving parents more actively in childcare facilities. The English report in the TSFEPS Project emphasizes the pedagogical philosophy of early excellence centres (EECs) that try to involve parents in the daily activities of childcare facilities and the Belgium report refers to policies to mobilize parents. Such pedagogical efforts are related to special social goals of integrating and empowering resource weak groups of parents in these two countries.

Parent associations, initiatives and co-operatives in France, Germany and Sweden are both managed and maintained by the parents themselves. But very few examples exist of direct, systematic parent involvement in the pedagogical aspects of childcare in such facilities. Rather parents provide a necessary complement to the professional staff. Parents can substitute for professional staff when the latter are absent due to sickness or relieve them for other reasons, such as attending training courses, etc. The presence of parents at a childcare facility can also enrich the environment of childcare facilities. In particular, the presence of fathers, in an otherwise heavily female-dominated occupation group is positive both for young boys and girls. However, parent involvement in parent-run facilities is normally confined to performing non-professional tasks related to running and managing the facility, the maintenance and repairs, keeping the books, contacts with the authorities and cooking occasionally. Thus, there is little risk that non-professional parents will permanently substitute and finally replace professional staff in parent associations, initiatives and co-operatives. Rather there is a clear division of labour between the staff and parents.

Social participation can take several forms. Regular meetings of parents can facilitate the creation of parent networks. Parents can be charged with helping to organize or arranging various social events, like the Christmas party, the end of the year party in June, etc. Such events can either be limited to those directly associated with the childcare facility, i.e. the staff, parents and children; or they can be open to residents of the neighbourhood where the childcare centre is located. In the latter case they also involve the childcare centre's social relations in the neighbourhood. Some country reports stress that municipal childcare services prefer to limit parties and festivals to the children, staff and parents of the facility, while parent initiatives and co-operatives prefer to see childcare as a way of integrating families into the social life of the neighbourhood (Evers and Riedel 2003; Fraisse and Bucolo 2003; Lhuillier 2003).

The case studies analysed here demonstrate a wide range of patterns of parent participation. At the aggregate level, participation can either be *ad hoc* or it can take more corporatist forms of representation of various stakeholders in city-wide consultative bodies charged with developing childcare services. The latter is normally the case when a variety of different stakeholders exist in the same geographical context, the welfare mix is accepted by most actors and no single form of production dominates the provision of childcare services. Some cities included in our eight-country study demonstrated a form of corporatist representation in permanent consultative bodies for all major providers of childcare services, while others did not. Institutions for regular city-wide consultation between various service providers may be seen as the co-management of a sector. Regular consultation with most or all of the providers may also be prescribed by law, as seen in some of the TSFEPS countries (Evers and Riedel 2003; Fraisse and Bucolo 2003; Lhuillier 2003). *Ad hoc* consultations may take place in a city where the municipal government normally dominates the provision of such services. Once the number of non-municipal providers grows beyond a certain level they may be consulted in an *ad hoc* fashion. This is illustrated in Sweden by the existence of such consultations in Stockholm and Gothenburg, but not Östersund. However, such consultations are not required by law (Strandbrink and Pestoff 2006).

Turning to the level of the individual childcare services, participation took quite different forms. Most childcare services studied here fall into the top – down category in terms of style of service provision. There are few possibilities for parents to influence decision making directly in such services. This normally includes both municipal childcare services and for-profit firms providing childcare services in the countries studied here. Perhaps this is logical from the perspective of municipal governments. They are, after all, representative institutions, chosen by the voters in elections. They might consider direct client or user participation in the running of public services for a particular group, like parents, a threat both to the representative democracy they institutionalize and to their power. It could be argued that direct participation for a particular group would thereby provide them with a veto right or a second vote at the service level. There may also be professional considerations for resisting parent involvement and participation.

The logic of direct participation is also foreign to private for-profit providers. Exit, rather than voice provide the medium of communication in markets, where parents are seen as consumers. This logic excludes any form of indirect or direct representation. Only the parent associations, initiatives and co-operatives noted in some country reports clearly fall into the bottom – up category. Here we find the clearest examples of self-government and direct democracy. Parents are directly involved in the running of their daughter and/or son's childcare centre in terms of being responsible for the maintenance, management, etc. of the childcare facility. They also participate in the decision making of the facility, as members and owners of the facility.

SUMMARY AND CONCLUSIONS ABOUT CO-PRODUCTION OF CHILDCARE

I will now consider the implications of these findings for the development of the concept of co-production and then discuss their implications for the contribution of co-production to the development and renewal of democracy and the welfare state. We find an attempt to identify various types of citizen participation in terms of co-production resulted in examples of direct contributions in economic, political, pedagogical and social terms by parents to the value created by childcare facilities throughout Europe. However, some forms of participation seem more germane than others in terms of co-production. Some of the activities mentioned earlier could perhaps better be classified as auxiliary or ancillary activities, rather than co-production. In particular many of the pedagogical and social activities appear to be of this nature. They are normally part of collective childcare regardless of the country or provider. However, both the economic activities found in Bulgaria, as well as the management and decision-making activities by parents found in parent associations, initiatives and co-operatives in France, Germany and Sweden, qualify as co-production. However, we should consider whether they might possibly be classified as parallel production.

The main reason for not classifying them as parallel production is that these childcare services are financed by public funds. Moreover, the parent associations, initiatives and co-operatives found in France, Germany and Sweden are contributing to the fulfilment of public goals of providing childcare services to as many parents as possible and in a form that parents not only approve, but are willing to contribute with their time and effort. In Sweden childcare is now an entitlement for all children between the ages of one and six years old. If the parents did not make contributions of their time and effort to alternative providers or if the latter did not exist, then these same parents would demand public services. The public authorities would be obliged to provide them; but they might be hard pressed to do so. Thus, although alternative services are provided by separate organizations, they are both financed by public funds and they contribute to fulfilling public policy goals in this area.

Ostrom's discussion of co-production in terms of production functions notes that it may involve strictly substitutable or complementary processes. Substitution would imply parallel production and involve parent participation in all areas of pre-school, including pedagogical activities, not just in some tasks. Parent participation, primarily in the maintenance and management of childcare facilities, comprise complementary activities that create synergies based on a clear division of labour between the professionals and parents. Here the parents take over the secondary activities, while the professionals can concentrate on their core ones, the pedagogy of pre-school learning.

Alternative provision of childcare for pre-school children comprises an interesting example of co-production in France, Germany and Sweden. Public financing is available to all types of childcare providers in Sweden; e.g. public, private for-profit and third-sector childcare. However, only the latter appear to facilitate extensive parent participation. Today approximately 15 per cent of all pre-school aged children are enrolled in third-sector childcare in Sweden.

Moreover, co-production appears to change its form with changed conditions. Initially co-production referred to the degree of overlap between two sets of participants in the service production process – regular producers and consumers. The resulting overlap represents the joint effort of these two groups, both public professionals and citizens, in the provision of public services. It was not necessary that they be organized in the same organization. However, with today's system of contracting out and the growing welfare mix, we need to recognize that citizens can participate in various ways. They can participate on either an individual or organized basis in the provision of neighbourhood safety in the USA, or in permanent organized groups of users at third-sector organizations providing welfare services in Europe. The latter would include participation in parent associations, initiatives and co-operative childcare services found in France, Germany and Sweden. In the former case users are clearly a complement to professional public providers of neighbourhood safety, i.e. the police. In the latter case citizens take over the management of welfare services, but the public sector still finances and supervises the provision. This would imply an extension of the concept of co-production to include collective efforts to provide public financed services produced by third-sector providers. The two main requirements for co-production are the continued public financing of such services and the participation of consumer producers or citizens in their provision.

Finally, the term co-production needs to be distinguished from similar, but different phenomena of co-management and co-governance. The growing welfare mix and diversity of providers not only implies greater citizen involvement in the provision of some public financed services, but it also becomes necessary to manage and govern this growing diversity. Co-management refers to the growing diversity or hybridization of providers of welfare services, typically found in situations where NPOs and/or FPOs participate in the provision of public financed services (Brandsen 2004), with or without greater citizen involvement at the site of production. Co-governance refers to attempts to manage this growing diversity in a more democratic fashion through the creation of city-wide, provincial and/or national bodies where various providers are represented and given a voice in governing the development of a sector. The appropriate site for co-governance structures will depend, of course, on constitutional differences between various welfare states. We found some examples of this in the childcare sector in France and Germany, but not Sweden, in spite of the growing diversity of providers of such services in all three countries. However, here we must also distinguish between consultations, no matter how frequent or structured, and decision making. Organizational participation in consultations may or may not lead to mutual adjustment, but this differs greatly from participation in binding decisions. Co-governance requires real input and influence in the development of a sector or provision of welfare services. This may be difficult to achieve without the existence of necessary intermediate structures among various providers of welfare services. This is particularly important for small third-sector providers, who may find it hard to organize themselves.

In conclusion, I will turn my attention to the implications of co-production for the development and renewal of democracy and the welfare state. Co-production provides a necessary conceptual tool for understanding citizen participation at the micro level or site of production of welfare services. It gives us a missing piece of the puzzle of democratic reform. It also underlines the importance of motivating and involving both the citizens and professionals in the process of institutional change. At the same time the political process is very important. Without the necessary political support and proper institutional structures little progress will be made.

However, we found that some dimensions of co-production in childcare appear more germane to the development and renewal of democracy and the welfare state than others. In particular the contribution of time by parents to the political dimension, noted earlier, promotes these goals more clearly than the economic, pedagogical or social dimensions. New ways need to be developed to encourage the participation of several different stakeholders in the provision of childcare services, not just a single one, as today. The staff, parents and financers of childcare services need to form multi-stakeholder organizations at the site of service production. Also institutions should be created by the authorities to promote greater participation by alternative or third-sector providers in the city-wide management of childcare services. This would, of course, require a change in the laws of most European countries. However, participation in childcare services should not be seen as a 'zero-sum' game or winner-take-all situation, but rather one where various stakeholders can make a contribution to better quality childcare through dialogue and co-operation with each other. Therefore they all deserve recognition of their potential contribution to a common goal. This recognition needs to be accompanied by providing them with ways and means for gaining influence in the day-to-day decisions of a childcare facility and the overall running of such services and the management of such services, both at the site of production and city-wide level.

This corresponds with calls by Walzer (1988), Hirst (1994) and Barber (2003 [1984]), along with many others for developing and renewing democracy and the welfare state. In particular, they call for providing welfare services through greater citizen involvement and a greater role for the third sector. The state has grown rapidly in recent decades and become part of an organizational society, where large organizations dominate both in the public and private sectors. However, they do not see this as contradictory with democracy or simply as calling for the withdrawal of the state. Rather they see it as enhancing the role of the state, by concentrating on financing and regulation of the provision of welfare services. Walzer notes the need for a strong state that can superintend and subsidize the work of its citizens, volunteers and third-sector organizations that provide welfare services. Hirst's Associative Democracy means devolving as many functions of the state as possible to the organizations of civil society in order to develop and renew democracy and curb the growth and dominance of big organizations, both in business and government.

However, without a clear idea of how to involve citizens in these sweeping reforms little progress can be made. Co-production provides a focus on citizens' participation at the level of local production of welfare services or the site of production. Co-production opens up possibilities for better understanding the importance of obtaining the consent and support of all three major stakeholders in such reforms, i.e. the citizens, the professional providers of welfare services and the politicians. However, without a clear vision of a 'good society', or at least a better society than today, it will be very difficult to promote such sweeping reforms. Co-production provides a missing piece of the puzzle for developing and renewing democracy and the welfare state.

Various aspects of co-production were explored and illustrated by childcare here, but it can also be found in other areas of welfare services. It exists today in different areas like education, eldercare, handicap care and health and medical care. Parent-run and managed elementary and high schools are found in many countries, sometimes in combination with a special pedagogical approach, like Waldorf or Montessori, and sometimes when public provision fails. Third-sector eldercare and other support groups provide alternatives in a rapidly growing field. Here children and relatives can become co-producers of some of the services provided to their parents and loved-ones (Dahlberg 2004). The Independent Living movement is spreading in many countries and provides much greater influence for families and handicapped persons than either public or private for-profit services (Westin 2006). Self-help groups in areas like diabetes and HIV/AIDS are a good example of co-production in health care (Walden Laing 2001; Söderholm Werkö 2006). Health care co-ops in Japan and elsewhere illustrate the possibility for informed and active members who want to maintain their health and avoid becoming passive patients in traditional public health systems (Pestoff 2006). Thus, the concept of co-production provides us with a better understanding of fundamental relations at the site of production of welfare services and a clearer comprehension of the dynamics of developing and renewing democracy and the welfare state.

ACKNOWLEDGEMENT

An earlier version of this work was presented to the Study Group on the Third Sector at the European Group for Public Administration, EGPA, in Ljubljana, Slovenia in

2004. I am grateful to comments there by Profs Stephen Osborne, Wim van der Donk, Tack Brandson and by co-panelists. Thanks also to anonymous reviewers for helpful critiques.

NOTES

1 See www.emes.net for more details and the country reports.
2 Only one city was included in England.

REFERENCES

Alford, J. (2002) Why Do Public Sector Clients Co-Produce? Towards a Contingency Theory, *Administration & Society*. 34: 1 pp32 – 56.

Barber, B. (2003 [1984]) *Strong Democracy: Participatory Politics for a New Age*, Berkeley, CA: University of California Press.

Brandsen, T. (2004) *Quasi-Market Governance: An Anatomy of Innovation*, Utretch: Lemma Publishing.

Brudney, J. (1984) Local Coproduction of Services and the Analysis of Municipal Productivity, *Urban Affairs Quarterly*. 19: 4 pp465 – 84.

Brudney, J. and England, R. (1983) Towards a Definition of the Co-Production Concept, *Public Administration Review*. 43: 1 pp59 – 65.

Dahlberg, L. (2004) *Welfare Relationships: Voluntary Organisations and Local Authorities in Supporting Relatives of Older People in Sweden*, PhD dissertation. Studies in Politics, no. 101. Stockholm.

Galbraith, J. K. (1984) *The Anatomy of Power*, London: Hamish and Hamilton.

—— (1986) 'Power and Organizations' in S. Lukes (ed.) *Power*. London: Basil Blackwell.

Häggroth, S. (2005) *Staten och Kommunerna [The State and Municipalities]*, Sthlm, SOU: Ansvarskommittén.

Hirst, P. (1994) *Associative Democracy: New Forms of Economic and Social Governance*, Cambridge: Polity Press.

—— (2002) 'Democracy and Governance' in J. Pierre (ed.) *Debating Governance, Authority, Steering and Democracy*. Oxford: Oxford University Press.

Ostrom, E. ed. (1975) *The Delivery of Urban Services: Outcomes of Change*, Beverly Hills, CA: Sage.

—— (1999) 'Crossing the Great Divide: Coproduction, Synergy, and Development' in M. McGinnis (ed.) *Polycentric Governance and Development: Readings from the Workshop in Political Theory and Policy Analysis*. Ann Arbor, MI: University of Michigan Press.

Parks, R. B., Baker, P. C., Kiser, L., Oakerson, R., Ostrom, E., Ostrom, V., Percy, S. L., Vandivort, M. B., Whitaker, G. P. and Wilson, R. (1981) Consumers as Co-Producers of Public Services: Some Economic and Institutional Considerations, *Policy Studies Journal*. 9 pp1001 – 11. Reprinted in McGinnis, M. ed. (1999) *Local Public Economies: Readings from the Workshop in Political Theory and Policy Analysis*. Ann Arbor, MI: University of Michigan Press.

Percy, S. (1984) Citizen Participation in the Co-production of Urban Services, *Urban Affairs Quarterly*. 19: 4 pp431 – 46.

Pestoff, V. (1999 [1998]) *Beyond the Market and State: Social Enterprises and Civil Democracy in a Welfare Society*, Aldershot, Brookfield, NJ & Singapore: Ashgate.

—— (2006) Democratizing Health Care – the Japanese Example. Paper presented at the European Group on Public Administration, Study Group on the Third Sector, September, Milan.

Peters, G. (1994) Alternative Models of Governance: The Changing State of Public Service. Paper presented at the IPSA Congress, RC27, August, Berlin. Published (1996) as *The Future of Governing: Four Emerging Models*, Lawrence, KS: University Press of Kansas.

Rich, R. C. (1981) Interaction of Voluntary and Governmental Sectors: Towards an Understanding of Co-Production of Municipal Service, *Administration & Society*. 13: May pp59 – 76.

Rosentraub, M. and Warren, R. (1987) Citizen Participation in the Production of Urban Services, *Public Productivity Review*. 41 pp75 – 89.

Sharp, E. B. (1980) Towards a New Understanding of Urban Services and Citizen Participation: The Co-Production Concept, *Midwest Review of Public Administration*. 14: June pp105 – 18.

Strandbrink, P. and Pestoff, V. (2006) 'Small Scale Welfare on a Large Scale: Social Cohesion and the Politics of Swedish Childcare.' Research report 2006:5, Huddinge: Södertörns högskola.

Söderholm Werkö, S. (2006) 'Patient Patients? Patient Empowerment through Patient Organizations.' Stockholm: School of Business, Stockholm University.

Walden Laing, D. (2001) 'HIV/AIDS in Sweden and the United Kingdom Policy Networks 1982 – 1992.' Studies in Politics, no. 81, Stockholm: Stockholm University.

Walzer, M. (1988) 'Socializing the Welfare State' in A. Gutmann (ed.) *Democracy and the Welfare State*. Princeton, NJ: Princeton University Press.

Warren, R., Harlow, K. and Rosentraub, M. (1982) Citizen Participation of Services: Methodological and Policy Issues in Co-Production Research, *Southwestern Review*. 2: 41 – 55.

Westin, A. (2006) 'Med Rätt att Bestämma Själv?' [Deciding on Your Own?] (A Comparison of Public, Private-for-Profit and Nonprofit Providers of Handicap Care in Sundsvall), Östersund: Mid-Sweden University.

Whitaker, G. (1980) Co-production: Citizen Participation in Service Delivery, *Public Administration Review*. 40: 3 pp240 – 6.

TSFEPS reports

The TSFEPS Project, Changing Family Structures and Social Policy: Childcare Services as Sources of Social Cohesion, took place in eight European countries between 2002 – 4. They were Belgium, Bulgaria, England, France, Germany, Italy, Spain and Sweden. See www.emes.net for more details and the reports.

Evers, A. and Riedel, B. (2003) 'Governance and Social Cohesion in Childcare: The Example of Frankfurt and München.' Giessen: Justus-Liebig-Universität.

Fraisse, L. and Bucolo, E. (2003) 'TSFEPS Etude de Cas – France.' Paris: CRIDA.

Lhuillier, V. (2003) 'TSFEPS – Études de Cas: Bruxelles – Schaerbeek et Ottignies – Louvain la Neuve.' Universite Catholique de Louvain: CERISIS.

Strandbrink, P. and Pestoff, V. (2003) 'Small Children in a Big System: A Case Study of Childcare in Stockholm and Östersund.' Östersund: Södertörns högskola; Huddinge & Mid-Sweden University.

CHILDCARE, CO-PRODUCTION AND THE THIRD SECTOR IN CANADA

Susan Prentice

CHILDCARE, CO-PRODUCTION AND THE THIRD SECTOR IN CANADA

The history of childcare in Canada is largely a story of bad timing. Childcare had the misfortune of coming to the policy table late in the post-war period, well after the main features of social service provision in Canada had been laid down. Called 'daycare', 'nurseries' or 'creches' in its day, the service grew out of charitable philanthropy, and this history of residualism meant that childcare entered public policy as a welfare matter, rather than as a rights-based service like education. Worse, it became featured on the national agenda during an era of major retrenchment and restructuring. Despite this timing, all has not been hopeless. Even though national childcare policy progressed little throughout the 1980s and early 1990s – one observer called the period 'a lost two decades for childcare in Canada' (Lauziere 2004: 3) – movement stepped up rapidly after 2000.

In 2003, federal, provincial and territorial governments signed a Multilateral Framework Agreement on Early Learning and Care, following on the heels of an Early Childhood Development Agreement approved in 2000. In 2004, the Throne Speech acknowledged it was time for a 'truly national system of early learning and child care.' The federal government committed to a national childcare programme and in 2005, the first beginnings were laid down through a $5 billion/five-year initiative consisting of bilateral agreements with provinces and territories. The Throne Speech observed that there was an 'urgent need to accelerate development of quality early learning and child care across the country' and it proposed to address that need through a funding programme that met the principles of quality, universally inclusive, accessible and developmental care (Govt. of Canada 2004: 8).

These intentions, however, are quixotic. Canadian childcare is organized as a market-based service provided almost exclusively by commercial and third-sector entrepreneurs, a familiar pattern in liberal and residual welfare states (O'Connor *et al.* 1999). As a result, there is a significant disconnect between the newly announced national political vision for childcare and existing mechanisms for local implementation. Outside Quebec, a completed circuit for childcare from the national, through the provincial, to the local level has yet to be constructed. In consequence, a national system of early learning and childcare currently is structurally unobtainable. As the OECD (2004: 69) noted in its recent review of Canadian childcare, national and provincial policy is 'divided and incoherent'.

Most of Canada's centre-based childcare spaces are privately provided by the voluntary or commercial sectors. About four out of five childcare centre spaces in Canada are delivered by parents for parents, who both pay for the service as well as control it. The remaining 20 per cent of spaces are operated as commercial for-profit businesses where fee-paying parents are clients (Friendly and Beach 2005: 206). Childcare services provided directly by government make up less than one-tenth of the country's spaces, and are found in just two of Canada's ten provinces.[1] While the ratio of voluntary to for-profit care has shifted over time, the publicly operated sector has remained miniscule.

Childcare is a form of co-production, wherein services are initiated, delivered and maintained by parent-users and governments depend upon such non-state action for policy implementation. Such co-production, however, takes on a particular inflection. While it fits the general understanding of 'involvement by users in the production of the services they use', it sits more awkwardly with the assumption that co-production involves complementary relations with public services provided by the state. Unlike in more family-friendly and redistributive welfare states (such as the Nordic countries), co-production in childcare is neither a supplement to public provision nor involves government-to-citizen relations. Co-production in Canadian childcare, instead, is the result of the *absence* of public provision and government involvement. Further, despite the state's reliance on private agents to deliver childcare services, there are few-to-no mechanisms to integrate the sector into policy development, governance or service co-ordination. By the criteria developed by Brandsen and Pestoff (this issue), both co-governance and co-management are absent. Such is the context for a consideration of co-production and the third sector in Canadian childcare.

This contribution reviews the current configuration of market-based services that constitutes Canada's current childcare regime and considers its prospects. I conclude that the present architecture is unlikely to deliver universally accessible, high-quality childcare. Thus, there are some cautionary lessons from a review of childcare, co-production and the third sector. These lessons are drawn from Canadian experience, yet they also bear directly on other liberal states where instead of public provision and entitlement, childcare is provided by markets – whether informal, third-sector or for-profit.

CHILDCARE SERVICES IN CANADA

Despite robust evidence that 'childcare is smart social policy, smart economic policy and smart health policy' (Battle and Torjman 2002: 1) actual service belies this. Canada has just 745,254 licensed childcare spaces to serve 4.8 million children aged 0–12 years, providing coverage to 15.5 per cent of the country's youngsters (Friendly and Beach 2005). Like other social services, childcare falls under provincial and territorial jurisdiction. At the service delivery level, 'the bulk of the supply of regulated childcare is initiated and maintained by parent and/or voluntary boards of directors' (Friendly and Beach 2005: xviii). About 80 per cent of Canada's centre spaces are non-profit, delivered through the third sector. Only a very small portion of Canada's non-profit centre spaces are publicly operated, generally by municipalities (primarily in Ontario) or school boards (such as Quebec's school-age programmes) (Doherty *et al.* 2003: 28). Childcare in Canada is a patchwork of services characterized by inadequacy, fragmentation and incoherence. The Mayor of Toronto recently despaired that 'choice in child care does not exist for most Canadian families who want access to early learning in a regulated program' (Miller 2006: A-21).

Childcare is a market-based, user-pay service in Canada, financed through a mix of parent fees, subsidies paid on behalf of low-income families and some direct funding to programmes. Childcare is financed primarily through parent fees, which make up over half the annual budget of centres in 6 of 10 provinces, contributing 49.2 per cent of revenues for the country as a whole. Fees vary considerably by province and by the age of the child, often reaching well over $10,000 per child. The second major source of funding is fee subsidies paid by the provincial government on behalf of low-income families. Fee subsidies are severely limited, and families must generally be well under the poverty line to qualify. Parent fees and fee subsidies together make up 79.7 per cent of centre revenues. The remaining one-fifth of centre budgets is derived from direct funding. Government allocations per regulated space range from a low of $816/yr in Alberta to a high of $4,849/yr in Quebec, making up about 17.5 per cent of centre revenues nationally (Doherty *et al.* 2000: ch. 10; Friendly and Beach 2005: 188, Table 12). This national average masks dramatic inter-provincial differences: parent fees and subsidies make up 100 per cent of centre revenues in Newfoundland, for example, and 98 per cent in New Brunswick. Nationally, parent fees and fee subsidies make up $5 out of every $6 spent on regulated childcare in Canada, compelling evidence of the degree to which childcare is conceived of and delivered as a private service.

Outside of its minor funding role, state involvement is mainly regulatory. In most of Canada, childcare is delivered by citizens to citizens, as parents control the boards of facilities they initiate. In most centres, parents pay high fees as well as make voluntary contributions by serving on the board of directors, fundraising, donating materials or special skills and participating in pedagogical activities such as field trips and special celebrations (Prentice and Ferguson 2000). A very limited number of non-profit programmes also function as parent co-operatives, with formal expectations of parent involvement 'on the floor' (Killian 1972; Atkin 1998).[2] Despite near-absolute reliance on the third sector to deliver childcare, few provinces have developed formal mechanisms to integrate the sector into policy development or service co-ordination (Prentice 2004).

If the link between local service delivery and provincial policy and practice is tenuous, the interaction between sub-national and federal levels is even less developed. An institutional legacy of privatization and third-sector reliance poses distinct limits to federal policy capacity. For example, over 2005 the federal government of Liberal Prime Minister Paul Martin announced its intention to build a national system of early learning and care. Yet, in practical terms, the federal government has no capacity to deliver on this clarion call. Ottawa has no significant policy instrument to deploy because the provinces and territories have jurisdiction and pay the lion's share of government costs, leaving Ottawa with no direct policy or operational role (Battle and Torjman 2002).

THIRD-SECTOR TROUBLES

The Canadian practice of meeting public policy goals by delivering childcare services through the voluntary sector generates some advantages and greater disadvantages. As Smith and Lipsky (1993) have aptly observed, for conservatives the appeal of privatization is the promise of smaller government and more reliance on private initiative. To liberals, reliance on non-profit agencies can meet social problems previously borne by the affected individuals and their families without implying either wholesale public responsibility or full public cost. Moreover, non-profit and community-based organizations are seen as ways to protect and promote individual and family choices. There is an appeal to partnerships from the left, as well. Community-based services can offer 'bottom – up' local control that builds community capacity, combats bureaucracy and promotes social cohesion. Certainly, community-governed childcare services provide for significant user involvement and control (Prentice 2000b).

However, there is an associated set of disadvantages with the current privatized configuration in the context of near-exclusive private provision. In the following, I review those that most shape childcare policy and provision in Canada. Such a review is necessarily schematic and flattens important intra-provincial differences and historical developments. Despite these risks, an overview allows the foregrounding of important patterns and illuminates some of the little-studied issues raised by partnerships between the public and not-for-profit private sector.

FRUSTRATED NATIONAL AND PROVINCIAL POLICY CAPACITY

When the Canadian government announced its interest in establishing a national system of early learning and care in 2005, it ran straight into the limitations of social services under federalism. Constitutionally established divisions of power give authority over education and welfare to the provinces. In addition, what little capacity central government does have to establish programmes with national standards and portability rights has been severely diminished over recent years through decentralization. Under the 1999 Social Union Framework Agreement (SUFA), the federal government voluntarily formalized limits on the use of its spending power. SUFA was designed as a vehicle to finance cost-shared social programmes, promising renewal and national equity. Yet it also constrains the federal government from implementing any new social programme that does garner support from a majority of the country's ten provinces. In practice, what this has meant is that 'the federally dominated cooperative federalism of the past has given way to the partnership federalism of today in areas of provincial/territorial jurisdiction' (Battle and Torjman 2002: 13). SUFA expresses a new paradigm of federalism that minimizes the role of federal government, moving towards a *co-ordination* rather than a *leadership* role for Ottawa.

This political history explains why Canada does not now have, and is unlikely to implement, national childcare legislation – despite calls going back at least as far as the ground-breaking 1970 Royal Commission on the Status of Women. Instead, each of Canada's ten provinces and three territories, as well as the federal government, has its own approach to early childhood care and education. As a result, 'the range, quality and access to early childhood education and care services and access to them vary enormously by region and circumstances' (Friendly and Beach 2005: xv). The 'province-centred governance structure' has failed to create universally accessible, comprehensive, high-quality childcare for Canadians (Mahon 2004).

The logic of private-sector reliance leads to less, rather than more, public involvement. Such government inaction has the effect of locating childcare as something outside of public accountability (Bacchi 1999). Recent evidence of such positioning is the federal government's minimal conditions for provincial spending on childcare under the 2005 bilateral childcare agreements, and the even more extreme silence on auspice (who owns and operates the service). While two western provinces (Manitoba and Saskatchewan) voluntarily committed themselves to deploying their bilateral funds only on non-profit care, other provinces' agreements with the federal government contain no such intention. One province (Alberta) even negotiated the right to spend its childcare dollars on services other than regulated early learning and care.

Across Canada, childcare services are mainly provided by independent, stand-alone centres. Since it is not a 'system', there is no co-ordination within or between provinces on childcare policy development or service innovation. Unlike either the health or education fields, there is literally no infrastructure at local, provincial, regional or pan-Canadian scales. Yet, all organized social service systems (such as education and health) require a resourced infrastructure. Infrastructure (in the form of personnel, resources and authority) enables a sector to partake in policy development, to collaborate with sister organizations, to communicate effectively with members, to provide professional development and in-service opportunities, to conduct research and development projects, to monitor research findings for best practices, to scrutinize public programmes and spending and to launch public education campaigns. SUFA, for example, authorizes a vague 'public' to monitor federal and provincial spending – and yet there is no institutionalized vehicle to undertake this work on behalf of childcare.

The lack of infrastructure is consequential. For example, an absence of organized infrastructure marginalized the childcare sector in negotiations over the distribution of 2000 federal Early Childhood Development funds, which were designed as a cafeteria of programmes from which provinces could select options:

> Only ten percent of the over $300 million in federal funds was used for childcare. Only six of the 13 governments invested *any* of the money in childcare, and none of the biggest – Ontario, Alberta and British Columbia – did so.
>
> (Mahon 2004: 9)

The disbursement of Early Childhood Development funds reveals the lack of co-management and the 'disorganized' character of the voluntary sector.

A final element of frustrated policy capacity relates to the longstanding practice of prioritizing demand-side subsidies over supply-side investments. The current national

Conservative government is proposing a 'choice in childcare allowance' of $1,200 per child under age 6 years in lieu of direct funding to provinces under the bilateral agreements, at a total cost of $10.9 billion over 5 years. This is the most marked initiative in this direction, but its policy logic perfectly corresponds to privatized market delivery and governance. A long-established demand-side subsidy is the federal Child Care Expense Deduction, the regressive tax measure for forms of receipted children's caring expenses (regulated childcare as well as sports camps, childminding, etc.). In 2003, Finance Canada estimated the tax expenditure on this income tax measure to be $545 million (Government of Canada 2005: ch. 4). In its 2004 review of childcare, experts from the Organization for Economic Co-Operation and Development (OECD 2004) devoted considerable attention to critiquing Canada's reliance on demand-side subsidies over direct funding of services.

COMMERCIAL CHILDCARE

For-profit childcare facilities provide one in every five childcare centre spaces in Canada – a national total that has been diminishing for some years, but one that shows real potential to grow if federal funding becomes available (Cleveland and Krashinksy 2005).[3] Each of Canada's provinces permits for-profit childcare services to be licensed and eligible to varying degrees for public funds. The net result is that while most of Canada's centres are non-profit, in some jurisdictions there is also a sizeable for-profit sector. The proportion of for-profit care ranges from a high of 73 per cent in Newfoundland and Labrador to a low of zero in Saskatchewan, the North West Territories and Nunavut (Friendly and Beach 2005).

A growing research literature documents the clear trend of higher quality in non-profit childcare, in large part because of the tendency of for-profit programmes to 'skimp' on a wide range of quality indicators, including those associated with staff. For-profit childcare has a negative impact on staff qualifications and wage levels, training opportunities and staff/child ratios and in combination with other features of organizational behaviour, the empirical evidence of poorer quality is definitive (Child Care Resource and Research Unit n.d.; Schom-Moffat 1984, 1992; Kagan 1991; Phillips *et al.* 1992; Canadian Day Care Advocacy Association & Canadian Child Day Care Federation 1993; Doherty 1995; Whitebrook *et al.* 1998; Morris and Helburn 2000; Prentice 2000a; Mitchell 2002; Cleveland 2005).

Empirical concerns about quality in for-profit childcare are borne out in Canada by numerous studies. One such analysis was undertaken by Gordon Cleveland and Michael Krashinsky, who used the national 1998 *You Bet I Care!* dataset to examine quality differences between for-profit and non-profit programmes. They determined that non-profit centres score about 10 per cent higher in quality. They found, moreover, that for-profit centres are disproportionately represented among the lower-quality centres. Non-profit centres tend to have better ratios of children to staff and are more likely than for-profit centres to exceed minimum ratios. Lead teachers in non-profit classrooms have more training and experience. Staff wages are lower overall in commercial centres (about 25 per cent lower among lead teachers). Non-profit programmes serve a wider age of children (in particular, more infants) and more children from diverse economic backgrounds (including more children receiving a fee subsidy and more children with special needs). Cleveland and Krashinsky (2004: 13) conclude that 'the positive impact of non-profit status on quality is persistent, even when a wide range of variables is held constant'.

Similar findings about quality differentials between for-profit and not-for-profit programmes have been found even in Quebec's highly regarded system (Fournier and Drouin 2004a, 2004b; Japel *et al.* 2005). In Quebec, as elsewhere, although there are good and poor-quality programmes in both auspice categories, the pattern of distribution is remarkable. Non-profit infant programmes were six times more likely than for-profit programmes to offer high-quality care (providing good or very good care). Non-profit pre-school programmes were four times more likely than for-profit centres to be among the best programmes. For-profit centres were vastly over-represented among programmes that provided unsatisfactory care. For-profit infant centres were more than eight times more likely than non-profit centres to provide unsatisfactory quality. For-profit pre-school programmes were six times more likely than non-profits to provide unsatisfactory care (Prentice 2005: 8 – 10).

Empirical Canadian evidence demonstrates that where public policy and financing discourages for-profit childcare, the proportion of for-profit care is lower and the quality of care is higher; conversely, where legislation and funding supports for-profit childcare, the proportion of for-profit care is higher and the quality is lower. In environments sympathetic to for-profit care, the for-profit sector both finds and makes opportunities to entrench further its interests. Regulations play only a small role in tempering these associations: licensing and regulatory regimes set generally minimal floors, and even these are regularly breached. Policing and compelling minimum standards is costly to jurisdictions, and diverts funds from more proactive quality improvements. As the international trade climate changes, even this modicum of public involvement may become more difficult – corporations are likely to find themselves succeeding with legal arguments that public regulations and funding regimes impair their private profits. Yet all provinces license proprietary childcare, and the federal government entirely disregarded for-profit auspice in its bilateral agreements.

Persistent poor quality in the commercial private sector ought to have generated changes to the privatization architecture, but it has not. As Vaillaincourt Rosenau (2000: 223) points out, 'many vulnerable populations are not able to meet the skilled, critical purchaser requirement of the buyer-beware market'. This creates the conditions that lead some observers to argue that personal social services ought not to be open to for-profit delivery (Smith and Lipsky 1993).

GEOGRAPHIC INEQUITY

The degree of geographic inequity in childcare services in Canada is known mainly in broad, rather than specific, terms. Across provinces, the level of service access varies widely – from a high of serving 29.9 per cent of Quebec's children to a low of just 4.9 per cent of children in Saskatchewan (Friendly and Beach 2005: 205, Table 26). Moreover, even within provinces, there is denser childcare in urban centres than in rural, northern or remote communities. Nationally, in 2002 – 3, 30 per cent of pre-school-aged children in an urban centre were likely to be in a childcare centre, compared to 22 per cent of rural children (Bushnik 2006: 17). This pattern of distribution within and between provinces is not accidental, however, being a built-in feature of a system that relies on the spontaneous self-organization of community organizations or the 'invisible hand' of the market to deliver childcare service. Under the Canadian version of co-production, the role of government is mainly to license childcare facilities and provide fee subsidies to low-income parents, not to plan, start-up or deliver services. Save Ontario's municipally operated childcare programmes and Quebec's public planning, all of Canada's services are reactive responses to private-sector initiatives.

Detailed analyses of the spatial dimensions of childcare in Canada are uncommon, although they exist elsewhere (England 1996; Van Ham and Mulder 2005) As urban geographer Marie Truelove (1996: 93) has argued, geographical access to a service must be regarded as 'an important component of the effectiveness of that service'. Geographical access to childcare shapes the spatial choice set of parents and children. In 2003, a close study of Winnipeg found the distribution of childcare spaces was linked to neighbourhood affluence (Prentice and McCracken 2004). Winnipeg had a capacity of 16,749 spaces provided by 251 full-day childcare centres, 74 part-day nurseries and 295 family homes. Childcare services are not evenly distributed in Winnipeg. Some neighbourhoods have many more facilities than others – for example, relatively affluent and suburban wards have the largest number of facilities, while inner-city and more impoverished neighbourhoods are near the bottom. Some wards have many times more childcare spaces and types of care than others. The number of family daycare homes, for example, is three times higher in suburban Elmwood than it is in other wards.

Geographic inequity characterizes the distribution of childcare spaces in Winnipeg. The particular shape of this maldistribution results in less access for Winnipeg's poorer and inner-city children and better access for its more affluent children. The absence and distorted distribution of services in Winnipeg reveals the ineffectiveness of the current childcare regime. In his discussion of territorial justice, David Harvey (1973) emphasizes that social justice requires a just distribution, justly achieved. The childcare policy architecture in Winnipeg – like all of Canada, save Quebec – is indicted by its failure to achieve a just distribution, a consequence of privatized co-production.

Reliance on the private sector, mainly non-profits, to provide childcare services means that neighbourhoods high in social and other capital are at an advantage. Highly disadvantaged communities, which do not enjoy the same degree of social and other capital, are at a disadvantage. Where the not-for-profit private sector is poorly organized or where social capital is insufficient, self-initiated community-based services are scarce. Absent public planning mandates to ensure access, however, these communities will likely remain under served.

The under-servicing of marginalized communities is particularly troubling, since it results in vulnerable children having lesser access to childcare, despite its documented capacity to mitigate some of the disadvantages of family poverty. 'High-quality daycare centres increase children's linguistic, cognitive and social competencies, and has long-lasting benefits for children from low-income families. Investments in daycare for vulnerable children have large returns over time' (Kohen *et al.* 2002: 273). This does not imply a preference for targeted services, however, since quality childcare creates benefits for all children. It is, instead, the argument that childcare is at least as necessary in poorer communities as it is in more affluent ones, despite a spatial distribution, which works in the opposite direction.

Geographic inequity is a built-in feature of the privatized delivery of childcare services in Canada – and there is little apparent will to modify this delivery model. The bilateral accords signed in 2005 entirely fail to consider public-sector delivery or public planning, deferring to the established architecture, wherein provinces rely on the third sector for implementation.

The reality of geographic inequity also goes unrecognized in the current federal government's alternative plan to provide a cash 'choice in childcare allowance' to parents, by-passing what the Conservative Party regularly calls 'institutionalized childcare'. Among other concerns, cash allowances presume a market of services that scarcely yet exist. The Caledon Institute points out that providing cash or tax breaks to parents goes only so far, since,

> at the end of the day, there must be something for parents to purchase. If there is little or no investment in the supply of high quality childcare while at the same time the cash-for-care approach results in more parents looking for good childcare, then this service becomes increasingly scarce relative to the demand.
>
> (Battle and Torjman 2002: 11)

COMPULSORY ALTRUISM, GENDER AND THE TIME CRUNCH

The final dysfunction of the privatized market of childcare is experienced by parents at the point of local delivery. About 80 per cent of Canada's licensed childcare is delivered by the non-profit sector, where organizations are governed by independent boards of directors. Full legal and financial authority is vested in the boards of directors of these non-profit organizations, and boards are nearly wholly made up of parent-users. In addition to paying to use childcare services, parents are also required to manage them – and it is at this point that the challenges of co-production become stark.

Parent involvement and control in the childcare centre is a complex issue. Undeniably, parent control and management provides important opportunities for local and participatory democracy. Client-controlled services are responsive and accountable to users, by-passing many of the well-known dysfunctions of large bureaucracies (Ferguson 1985; Pestoff 1998). At the same time, there are distinct limits to parent control as it is currently practised, namely the coercive and gendered dimensions of requiring extensive voluntary commitments from the highly time-crunched community of working parents.

Nominally sex-neutral 'parent' volunteerism and involvement is disproportionately enacted by women, who participate in childcare at much greater rates than do men. Moreover, there also is a classed and raced dimension to women's volunteerism, as they attempt to mediate the contradictions of a 'motherhood mandate' that prescribes constant maternal presence (Finch 1984; Prentice and Ferguson 1997). Under a commendable commitment to 'parent involvement' in theory, voluntary-sector co-production requires parents to assume what in other jurisdictions are public responsibilities.

Parental involvement is widely presumed to improve the quality of care of services offered to children, although the exact mechanism for this is rarely explained (Mayfield 1990; Shimoni and Ferguson 1992). Whatever effect parent involvement may have on the quality of care, it is certainly true that parent involvement requirements are a disincentive to commercial daycare operators, who are generally unwilling to concede control or authority to parents. Provinces with strong requirements for parent volunteerism, therefore, tend to have a smaller supply of commercial daycare than provinces that are silent on this aspect of delivery. Despite the many benefits of limiting the proprietary sector, childcare is one of the few social services in which client participation regularly is made mandatory by provincial regulations. Although client involvement may be encouraged or desired in fields such as mental health, eldercare and health, the insistence that (some) parents *must* volunteer in childcare is inextricably linked to the long western history of seeing the parent/child relationship as one of private property, in which parents (read mothers) must assume responsibility.

The expectations of parent volunteers in childcare are enormous: they are called upon to run agencies and centres, to develop policies, to manage and supervise staff, to assume fiduciary control over sizeable annual budgets, to participate in daily care, to fundraise to make up for fiscal shortfalls and to show in myriad ways that they care, and are taking responsibility. Moreover, since most mothers use childcare because of labour force participation or education/training, the time demands of compulsory altruism are extracted from perhaps the most time-crunched members of society (Hoschild 1989, 1997). Thus, parental volunteerism in childcare cannot be considered freely offered. To the contrary, it is largely the 'discharging of duty, both overt and covert' (Prentice and

Ferguson 2000: 119). Under these circumstances, mothers' volunteerism in childcare is hardly to be held up as an example of the moral superiority and excellence of the third sector. What mothers (like all parents) lack is a publicly managed or delivered system in which volunteerism could be freely offered or withheld.

CONCLUSION

In Canada, most parents who use regulated childcare have direct influence as well as control over their childcare services. As members of boards of directors, they operate and manage just under four-fifths of Canada's stock of childcare programmes and their fees represent over four-fifths of total childcare spending. Beyond mere 'voice' (Hirschman 1970), parents have the authority to initiate, manage and even terminate their childcare programmes. Governments directly operate much less than one-tenth of the country's spaces, and fund just 17.5 per cent of the cost. Yet, political pronouncements and public policy largely fail to recognize this reality, with the recent round of promises to build a national 'early learning and childcare system for the 21st century' (Liberal Party of Canada 2004: 29) being just the latest example. Moreover, despite profound reliance on the third sector to start up and deliver services, there is little-to-no provision for involving the voluntary sector in policy development or system governance. As a 'system' of individual stand-alone facilities governed directly by users, childcare lacks effective intermediate scales of neighbourhood, municipal, regional or provincial infrastructure.

Canada's current childcare regime is characterized by frustrated national and provincial policy capacity, a high degree of commercial childcare, inequities in service distribution and the burdening of parent-users, particularly mothers. There is a childcare space for just 15.5 per cent of the country's youngsters under the age of 12 years. Childcare suffers from a number of absolute shortfalls: Canadian childcare, as the OECD (2004: 69) experts observed, is best characterized as a fragile patchwork of fragmented services, severely stressed on the financing, access, equity and quality fronts. This overview demonstrates that Canada's history of looking to the third sector, in the absence of public delivery, has fundamentally failed Canadian children and their parents.

What would be the best way to ensure that Canada has a high-quality, universally accessible system of inclusive and developmental childcare? The political, inter-governmental, fiscal, policy, delivery and governance answers to this question are still open. What seems certain, however, is that the current form of third-sector co-production has little chance of succeeding.

In recent political and media controversies over childcare, opponents have objected to 'institutionalized' childcare, sometimes even calling it 'soviet style day care' (Piatkowski 2006: 38). Yet the paradox is that childcare in Canada is not 'institutionalized' at all, at least not in the sense usually implied by the term. To the contrary, childcare services exist in Canada mainly due to the extraordinary efforts of parents in the voluntary sector. Despite enormous challenges – summed up by government practices premised on the assumption that childcare is essentially a private- or voluntary-sector responsibility – third-sector initiatives have built what stands as Canada's childcare system.

This third-sector reliance is unstable and increasingly untenable. As more women enter the labour force and more parents seek out the benefits of early childhood care for their young children, childcare services are under increasing pressure for expansion. Yet the establishment of new services only occurs when communities self-organize to deliver non-profit care or when entrepreneurs open new commercial operations. Neither is a reliable basis for anticipating a national system of high-quality early learning and care, and neither is likely to lead to the acceleration of services called for in recent Throne Speeches.

Childcare advocates have long called for childcare to be reconceived as a public good, supported by public funding (Child Care Advocacy Association of Canada 2004). The movement of parents and allies is struggling to re-frame childcare as an entitlement. At a time when calls for public service are decried as 'etatist', childcare advocates are actively working to claim space on the public agenda. Such social movement activism for childcare contests deeply entrenched political, fiscal and social Canadian norms and welfare state practices. Despite the many troubles with third-sector reliance and the absence of public provision, the campaign to reform Canadian childcare faces steep odds.

ACKNOWLEDGEMENT

An earlier version of this article was presented to the session on 'The Third Sector, Co-Production and the Delivery of Public Services' at the Tenth International Research Symposium on Public Management, in Glasgow, April 2006. I am grateful to session organizers, Dr Victor Pestoff and Dr Taco Bransden for careful comments, and to co-panelists and audience members for their lively discussion and questions. Thanks to anonymous reviewers for their helpful critiques.

NOTES

1 It is estimated that about 10 – 15 per cent of the stock of non-profit spaces are publicly operated. In Ontario, childcare may be delivered by a municipality. In Quebec, school boards may operate school-age care (Doherty *et al.* 2003: 28).

2 The zenith of the co-op daycare movement was the 1970s, and has declined steadily since then.

3 Pestoff (1998) notes that even social democratic and family-friendly Sweden saw 'a three-fold growth' in commercial childcare after its 1992 decision to register private for-profit or commercial childcare. It should be noted that in the same period, co-operative and non-profit care also expanded, complementing well-established public-sector provision to positive effect (see Pestoff 1998).

REFERENCES

Atkin, W. (1998) 'Babies of the World Unite: The Early Day-Care Movement and Family Formation in the 1970s' in L. Chambers and E.-A. Montigny (eds) *Family Matters: Papers in Post-Confederation Family History*. Toronto: Canadian Scholars Press.

Bacchi, C. L. (1999) *Women, Policy and Politics: The Construction of Policy Problems*, London & Thousand Oaks, CA: Sage.

Battle, K. and Torjman, S. (2002) *Architecture for National Child Care*, Ottawa: Caledon Institute on Social Policy.

Bushnik, T. (2006) *Child Care in Canada: Research Paper*, Children and Youth Research Paper Series, Ottawa: Statistics Canada.

Canadian Day Care Advocacy Association & Canadian Child Day Care Federation (1993) *Caring for a Living: A Study on Wages and Working Conditions in Canadian Child Care*, Ottawa: Canadian Day Care Advocacy Association & Canadian Child Day Care Federation.

Child Care Advocacy Association of Canada (2004) *From Patchwork to Framework: A Child Care Strategy for Canada*, Ottawa: Child Care Advocacy Association of Canada.

Child Care Resource and Research Unit (n.d.) *What Does Research Tell Us about Quality in Child Care?*, Toronto: University of Toronto, Child Care Resource and Research Unit.

Cleveland, G. (2005) *The Non-Profit Advantage: Producing Quality Childcare in Thick and Thin Child Care Markets*, Toronto: University of Toronto at Scarborough, Division of Management.

Cleveland, G. and Krashinsky, M. (2004) *The Quality Gap: A Study of Nonprofit and Commercial Childcare Centres in Canada*, Toronto: Child Care Resource and Research Unit.

—— (2005) 'Why Harper's Child-Care Plan Won't Work.' *Toronto Star*, 13 May 2005.

Doherty, G. (1995) *Quality Matters: Excellence in Early Childhood Programs*, Don Mills: Addison-Wesley.

Doherty, G., Friendly, M. and Beach, J. (2003) *OECD Thematic Review of Early Childhood Education and Care: Canadian Background Report*, Ottawa: Government of Canada.

Doherty, G., Lero, D. S., Goelman, H. and Tougas, J. (2000) *You Bet I Care: A Canada-Wide Study on Wages, Working Conditions and Practices in Child Care Centres*, Guelph, ON: Centre for Families, Work and Well-Being, University of Guelph.

England, K. ed. (1996) *Who Will Mind the Baby? Geographies of Child Care and Working Mothers*, London: Routledge.

Ferguson, K. (1985) *The Feminist Case against Bureaucracy*, Philadelphia, PA: Temple University Press.

Finch, J. (1984) The Deceit of Self-Help: Pre-School Playgroups and Working Class Women, *Journal of Social Policy*. 13: 1 pp5 – 18.

Fournier, C. and Drouin, C. (2004a) *Educational Quality in Childcare Centre Daycares (Installations de CPE): Highlights, Summary Report No. 1*, Quebec: Government of Quebec.

—— (2004b) *Educational Quality in Private Daycares (Installations de CPE): Highlights, Summary Report No. 3*, Quebec: Government of Quebec.

Friendly, M. and Beach, J. (2005) *Early Childhood Education and Care in Canada, 2004*, Toronto: Child Care Resource and Research Unit, University of Toronto.

Government of Canada (2004) *Speech from the Throne to Open the First Session of the Thirty-Eighth Parliament of Canada*. Government of Canada, Ottawa. p8.

—— (2005) *Early Learning and Child Care Activities and Expenditures: Government of Canada Reports, 2003 – 2004*, Ottawa: Government of Canada Social Union.

Harvey, D. (1973) *Social Justice and the City*, London: Edward Arnold.

Hirschman, A. (1970) *Exit, Voice and Loyalty: Responses to Decline in Firms, Organizations and States*, Cambridge: Cambridge University Press.

Hoschild, A. (1989) *The Second Shift: Working Parents and the Revolution at Home*, New York: Viking.

—— (1997) *The Time Bind: When Work Becomes Home and Home Becomes Work*, New York: Metropolitan Books.

Japel, C., Tremblay, R. and Cote, S. (2005) Quality Counts! Assessing the Quality of Daycare Services Based on the Quebec Longitudinal Study of Child Development, *IRPP Choices*. 11: 5 pp3 – 42.

Kagan, S. (1991) Examining Profit and Nonprofit Child Care: An Odyssey of Quality and Auspice, *Journal of Social Issues*. 47 pp87 – 104.

Killian, M. (1972) 'Children are Only Littler People. Or, The Louis Riel University Family Coop' in Collective (ed.) *Women Unite*. Toronto: Women's Press.

Kohen, D., Hertzman, C. and Willms, D. (2002) 'The Importance of Quality Child Care' in D. Willms (ed.) *Vulnerable Children: Findings from Canada's National Longitudinal Survey of Children and Youth*. Edmonton and Ottawa: University of Alberta Press & HRD Canada.

Lauziere, M. (2004) Childcare for a Change, *Perception*. 27: 1–2 pp3 – 6.

Liberal Party of Canada (2004) *Moving Canada Forward: Foundations – A National Early Learning and Child Care Program*, Canada: Liberal Party of Canada.

Mahon, R. (2004) Early Child Learning and Care in Canada: Who Rules? Who Should Rule? Paper presented at 'Childcare for a Change', Third National Conference on Childcare in Canada, Canadian Council on Social Development, November, Ottawa.

Mayfield, M. (1990) 'Parent Involvement in Early Childhood Programs' in I. Dovey (ed.) *Child Care and Education: Canadian Dimensions*. Toronto: Nelson Canada.

Miller, D. (2006) 'Don't Kill National Child Care Plan.' *Toronto Star*.

Mitchell, L. (2002) *Differences between Community-Owned and Privately-Owned Early Childhood Education and Care Centres: A Review of Evidence*, NCZER Occasional Paper, Wellington, NZ: New Zealand Council for Educational Research.

Morris, J. and Helburn, S. (2000) Child Care Centre Quality Differences: The Role of Profit Status, Client Preferences and Trust, *Nonprofit and Voluntary Sector Quarterly*. 29: 3 pp377 – 99.

O'Connor, J., Orloff, A. S. and Shaver, S. (1999) *States, Markets, Families: Gender, Liberalism and Social Policy in Australia, Canada, Great Britain and the United States*, Cambridge: Cambridge University Press.

OECD (2004) *Canada: Country Note – Early Childhood Education and Care Policy*, Paris: OECD Directorate for Education, Organisation for Economic Co-operation and Development.

Pestoff, V. (1998) *Beyond the Market and the State: Social Enterprises and Civil Democracy in a Welfare Society*, Aldershot, Brookfield, NJ, Singapore & Sydney: Ashgate.

Phillips, D. A., Howe, C. and Whitebrook, M. (1992) The Social Policy Context of Child Care: Effects on Quality, *American Journal of Community Psychology*. 20: 1 pp25 – 51.

Piatkowski, S. (2006) 'It's Time To Put Down Our Rhetorical Crutches.' *Echo Weekly*, 15 – 21 June.

Prentice, S. (2000a) 'The Business of Child Care: The Issue of Auspice' in L. Prochner and N. Howe (eds) *Early Childhood Care and Education in Canada: Past, Present and Future*. Vancouver: University of British Columbia Press.

—— (2000b) 'The Case for Community-Governed Child Care Services' in G. Cleveland and M. Krashinsky (eds) *Our Children's Future: Child Care Policy in Canada*. Toronto: University of Toronto Press.

—— (2004) Manitoba's Childcare Regime: Social Liberalism in Flux, *Canadian Journal of Sociology*. 29: 2 pp193 – 207.

—— (2005) *For Profit Child Care: Past, Present, Future*, Occasional Paper no. 21, Toronto: Child Care Resource and Research Unit, University of Toronto.

Prentice, S. and Ferguson, L. (2000) 'Volunteerism, Gender and the Changing Welfare State: A Case Study in Child Day Care' in S. Neysmith (ed.) *Restructuring Women's Caring Labour: Discourse, State Practice and Everyday Life*. Toronto: University of Toronto Press.

Prentice, S. and McCracken, M. (2004) *Time for Action: An Economic and Social Analysis of Childcare in Winnipeg*, Winnipeg: Child Care Coalition of Manitoba.

Schom-Moffat, P. (1984) *The Bottom-Line: Wages and Working Conditions of Workers in the Formal Day Care Market*, Ottawa: Status of Women Canada, Task Force on Child Care.

—— (1992) *Caring for a Living: A Study of Wages and Working Conditions in Canadian Child Care*, Ottawa: Joint Project of the Canadian Child Day Care Federation and The Canadian Day Care Advocacy Association.

Shimoni, R. and Ferguson, B. (1992) Rethinking Parent Involvement in Child Care Programs, *Child and Youth Care Forum*. 21: 2 pp105 – 18.

Smith, S. R. and Lipsky, M. (1993) *Nonprofits for Hire: The Welfare State in the Age of Contracting*, Cambridge, MA: Harvard University Press.

Truelove, M. (1996) 'Minding the Baby in Canada' in K. England (ed.) *Who Will Mind the Baby? Geographies of Child Care and Working Mothers*. London: Routledge.

Vaillaincourt Rosenau, P. (2000) 'The Strengths and Weaknesses of Public – Private Partnership' in P. Vaillaincourt Rosenau (ed.) *Public – Private Partnerships*. Cambridge, MA: MIT Press.

Van Ham, M. and Mulder, C. (2005) Geographical Access to Childcare and Mothers' Labour-Force Participation, *Journal of Economic and Social Geography*. 96: 1 pp63 – 74.

Whitebrook, M., Howe, C. and Phillips, D. A. (1998) *Worthy Work, Unliveable Wages: The National Child Care Staffing Study, 1988 – 1997*, Washington, DC: Center for the Child Care Workforce.

CO-MANAGEMENT IN PUBLIC SERVICE NETWORKS

The organizational effects

Taco Brandsen and Eelco van Hout

INTRODUCTION

The third sector increasingly produces public services in collaboration with the state. In this collection, such an arrangement is referred to as *co-management*. Political rhetoric often suggests that this is a new phenomenon, but in fact such co-operation goes back a long way. What we now call the 'third sector' provided public services before the state ever did and in many countries its involvement in the welfare *state* dates back as far as the nineteenth century. It has not left the organizations in question unaffected. There is by now a wide range of literature documenting (and often lamenting) the transformation of informal, voluntary organizations to professional service deliverers. In this contribution, we will ignore the normative question whether the process of rationalization was good or bad in the first place, and look at the stage beyond. Recent research suggests that organizations involved in public service delivery are evolving towards forms of network production, in which the production process takes shape across a number of different organizations.

Various theories have been applied to this phenomenon, most notably the network theories that have been on the ascent in recent decades. Our analysis is indebted to this work and attempts to forge a tighter link with organizational theory. Network theory tends to conceptualize organizations as coherent entities, which is useful as an analytical method, but must be qualified by the observation that some of the problems associated with network integration are played out *within* organizations. The concept of co-management helps us to explore this phenomenon by linking interorganizational relations to the internal production process. As we will argue, organizations are faced with simultaneous pressures for differentiation and integration, which are alleviated (though not resolved) by internal changes in staffing, skills, structure and management style. Some of the problems of integrating public service networks are essentially resolved within organizations.

In our analysis, we will draw on empirical evidence from research projects in different fields of social policy:

- The results of the project 'Housing Association Diversification in Europe', an intensive case study analysis of social landlords in Ireland, Italy, the Netherlands and the UK, including thirty-five interviews with managers and stakeholders, and extensive documentation analysis.
- The results of the project 'Managing Hybrid Care Services', an intensive case study analysis of several levels of management in four providers of elderly care in the Netherlands, bases on forty interviews.
- The results of the project 'Local Care Networks: Meeting Local Care Demands', based on fifty interviews and extensive documentation analysis in local care and care-related organizations.

These studies do not constitute a representative sample and provide input for what is essentially an exploratory analysis. What we will arrive at are preliminary conclusions that require more systematic testing. To be clear about the nature of our case material, we have separated it from the main body of the text in the form of text boxes.

In the second section, we will describe the developments that have given rise to co-management, as well as our specific angle on these phenomena. The third section will describe tensions that arise within the networks within which service providers operate, which in turn may affect how they are internally organized. Accordingly, the fourth section describes several of such internal changes, e.g. in terms of staffing, skills and structure. The concluding fifth section discusses the broader implications of these findings for the concept of co-management.

MIXED MECHANISMS IN PUBLIC SERVICE DELIVERY

Public service delivery is not the exclusive territory of public administration, as it never really was. Modern governance implies that multiple parties are involved in the delivery of health care, elderly care, education, housing, welfare, safety and other public goods. Recent decades have been marked by a re-arrangement of the relationships between the state and third-sector organizations that supply public goods and services like education, housing, health care and community services. New third-sector organizations have been drawn into public service provision; in other words, there has been an increase in co-management between third sector and state. In addition, those third-sector organizations already in the public services have faced the challenges of quasi-marketization and/or performance measurement. Long-term relationships based on trust have been replaced by short-term, contract-based relationships, changing the nature of the government – third-sector partnership.

Broadly speaking, two types of effects can be discerned, one of integration and one of differentiation. It is one of the classic tensions of social science, which we will here approach primarily through the lens of organizational theory. In this context, differentiation denotes a rational division of labour, whereas integration refers to the co-ordination of interdependent activities (cf. Jaffee 2001). If an organization is to work effectively, then the two must be balanced. Any movement towards differentiation must be compensated by a movement towards integration. There is a lot of third-sector research documenting the effects of public contracting and regulation, imposed on groups and organizations when they apply for state funding. Such effects are usually conceived of in terms of rationalization, and more specifically bureaucratization.

At the level of organizations, it leads to a harder and more explicit social division of labour. The activities of organizations are redefined in terms of bureaucratic categories of action ('housing', 'welfare', etc.), which then become 'core tasks'. At the level of tasks, the process leads to a greater technical division of labour, with public goods disassembled into small and specialized components. For example, elderly care can be differentiated into different medical treatments (revalidation, different kinds of cure), into specific aspects of care (e.g. personal care, transport, home support), but also into the maintenance of buildings, treasury management and even staffing. This is a (perhaps inevitable) consequence of the effort to make services more accountable and more efficient.

There are several potential disadvantages of differentiation, such as the risk of asymmetric dependencies between parts of the system, the possibility that one element of the system may malfunction, conflicting interaction between the different parts and the costs of integration (Kenis 2006). Research on the third sector has tended to focus on the risks on asymmetric dependencies. As the system of public service delivery is further differentiated, there is a need for stronger mechanisms to integrate the various tasks (cf. Lawrence and Lorsch 1967). The different parts of the service delivery system must interact in such a way that they produce the desired outcome. The empirical evidence described in the next sections indicates that the opposite movement towards integration is initiated within the organizations themselves.

The movement towards integration that we are referring to takes the shape of linked production processes. Public services are increasingly delivered by networks rather than by single organizations and the integration of production processes is therefore closely linked to the integration of networks.

Our analysis has an obvious affinity with the network theories that have emerged in public management research (e.g. Klijn *et al.* 1995; Klijn 1996; Koppenjan and Klijn 2004). Much of this work is focused on the formation of networks (e.g. processes of framing, network activation) and the games played by actors in these networks (e.g. partnerships, selective activation). However, our conceptual starting-point differs from these and similar applications of network theory, which conceive of organizations as individual actors, connected to other individual actors. This is a useful analytical starting-point, especially when the focus is on processes at the network level and effective network management. However, there is the risk of losing sight of the fact that some of the dynamics of networks are played out below the network level. In the current analysis, we wish to draw attention to the relationship between network interactions and the internal organization. We will therefore wander purposefully in the border area between organizational and network theory. In that sense, our analysis is somewhat more closely related to studies on process management (e.g. de Bruijn *et al.* 2002) and on boundaryless organizations (Ashkenas *et al.* 2002).

Given that the involvement of third-sector organizations in public service delivery causes greater differentiation, and that this in turn causes a need for a compensating movement of integration, then the question for our analysis of co-management is how the latter is realized. Our focus in the current analysis will be primarily on third-sector organizations, given that they have been central to the empirical studies that underpin our argument. However, it may be possible to generalize our argument to other types of organizations. There are significant similarities between state, commercial and third-sector organizations active in the public services. In fact, they increasingly tend to become 'hybrid', without clearly belonging to any of these spheres.[1] The autonomy gained through such a hybrid position may in itself be one of the drivers of the integration process we have described. If hybridization is as important as we have claimed elsewhere (Brandsen and van Hout 2004; Brandsen *et al.* 2005) then our findings may be more widely relevant.

In any case, our findings show that co-management does not necessarily lead to a state of asymmetric dependence in which the autonomy of the third sector is lost. Many organizations appear to have taken important steps in rejuvenating welfare state policies from the bottom – up, attempting to resolve major tensions at the stage of policy implementation. The flipside is that it engenders a constant struggle over the coherence and identity of the organization.

RISING TENSIONS

The tension between differentiation and integration rises (or, to be more precise, sharpens) in relation to three aspects of third-sector organizations: external relations; accountability; and task demarcation.

External relations: Competition and co-operation

At the network level, the relationship between the different actors (state and third sector) involved in the production of services has become more ambiguous. On the one hand, they are increasingly in a situation where they are competitors (when the organizations address the same demands) or in a purchaser – provider relationship (e.g. when local authorities outsource part of the functions to other organizations). On the other hand, the products they make are often inextricably bound up, either as part of a chain or of a single geographical area. Patients often pass through different types of care; local communities are served by various organizations simultaneously. Efficiency and effectiveness, the objectives behind the reforms, also call for closer integration. This combined drive for competition and co-operation within a context of joint products places the managers of providers in a difficult position. The activities needed to achieve these two seem to be in direct conflict. Depending on the field in which providers are active, these conflicts appear to take different forms.

If services are produced in chains, as in health care, the integration of differentiated organizations is encouraged by transparent and interlocking organizational processes. One provider must pass on as much information about its clients to the next provider in the chain, so that care can be adapted to individual needs and the transition made as smooth as possible. This, in turn, requires a certain level of uniformity in administrative data and procedures, as well as openness regarding the treatments and other services clients have previously received. Competition, by contrast, favours distinctiveness and secrecy in relation to other providers. The aim of the game is to stay distinct. To give up one's distinctiveness or to share information about how it is achieved is to lose competitive advantage. This is an incentive for providers not to co-operate with other types of organizations active in their functional and/or geographical territory.

The same problem occurs when the relationship is one of purchaser and provider. Especially where innovation is concerned, which is long-term and risky, a certain extent of certainty is required. Yet the need to abide by regulations for public procurement often makes such certainty hard to achieve, as it is formally impossible to create preferred-supplier relationships. There have been instances when providers invested in innovative schemes, in close co-operation with local authorities, only to be replaced at the implementation stage, where they lost out to cheaper competitors. In the end, such uncertainty may discourage long-term innovation.

Accountability

One trend is for co-management to result in a stronger structuration of the activities of service providers. This expresses itself most clearly in relation to accountability, where there has been a major shift towards output legitimacy. The number of performance indicators has grown rapidly over the past years. It is a by now well-studied phenomenon, as is the oft-heard complaint that we are heading for an 'audit society' (Power 1997). Employees and managers of service providers argue that they feel that they are often more occupied with justifying themselves than with performing their duties. Whether or not such complaints are justified we will not discuss here.

What is important to note for our argument is that accountability mechanisms often overlap and sometimes hardly seem to be co-ordinated. This is perhaps to some extent inevitable, given the multiplicity of objectives in the context of co-management. For instance, meeting the professional requirements of social services (e.g. to devote personal attention to clients) can be at odds with the requirement to be efficient. The economic requirement to increase the numbers of students in higher-education conflicts with the educational quality of universities, unless additional funds are made available – which is rarely the case. The ambiguous and conflicting nature of organizational goals was noted by organizational theorists as early as the 1950s and is certainly not particular to the context we are describing. However, the formalization of such goals through accountability mechanisms, established as a consequence of co-management, sharpens the potential conflicts between goals because it reduces the scope for balancing by means of consensus. It is therefore more likely to encourage 'loose coupling', in which coherence is sacrificed to deal with external pressures.

Task demarcation: Diversification and core tasks

The third and final tension manifests itself in how the organization defines its core tasks. In the context of state funding, such tasks are often defined on the basis of bureaucratic borderlines. From a top–down perspective, the borders are necessary for the protection of budgets and for a clear political and legal division of responsibilities. However, real demand clearly fails to fit within these niches. Citizens tend to have little regard for bureaucratic sensitivities and often address their demands to whichever organization they happen to be in touch with. While some progress has been made with 'one desk' policies, there remains a tension between the differentiation within public service delivery and the unitary, messy nature of demand.

We have observed that, given that service providers have sufficient autonomy, they start taking initiatives to reconcile this tension. Such initiatives may be presented as 'a focus on communities', 'demand-driven supply', 'putting the customer central', borrowing from market or third-sector discourse, or both. In terms of organizational theory, it comes down to a strategy of diversification, possibly (though not necessarily) accompanied by a cognitive change in how the problems they need to solve are framed.

Accordingly, in our case studies we observed that organizations start to expand into new areas of activity where they believed their clients could be served better. Either they invented and implemented these new activities themselves, or they started formal co-operation with providers in other fields or in other parts of the chain. In health care, hospitals branched out in domiciliary care, following patients further down the production line. Such diversification may even lead to a revision of the organizational mission. For example, in our case study of housing, the associations and foundations in question started out as landlords, who merely rented out their property, and gradually expanded into various forms of urban regeneration and community investment. They went beyond their original (bureaucratically defined) function and adopted a more holistic perspective, in which they would 'revitalize communities' or something similar, treating their housing stock as a means rather than an end. It led to a burst of creative energy within the organizations we examined.

But broadening the organizational scope is not without risks. First of all, it may lead to a conflict with conditions attached to public funding. What from one perspective is considered as 'integration' may be regarded as 'leaking' from another. Furthermore, it is not always clear that organizations are competent in the new ventures they undertake. There are many examples of commercial businesses branching out into areas where they lack the expertise to be successful; the third sector is not necessarily different. Finally, when innovation and creative energy are devoted to new activities, this may adversely affect their core production 'technology', which is supposedly their strength. None the less, it is interesting to note that partnership with the state does not invariably lead to a narrower definition of activities, as much of the literature suggests. We can only speculate at this point, but it seems that organizations that are successful at creating a mixed resource base can acquire more freedom than those that make themselves dependent on a single donor. This would be in line with the premises of resource dependency theory (cf. Pfeffer and Salancik 1978).

Case 1: Complexity and hybridity in Dutch elderly care

The Dutch elderly care sector consists of professional organizations that have gone through several transformations over time, as was the case in many other Western European countries. The variety among providers has greatly increased. The environment of elderly care providers not only consists of clients and the national state, but also of insurance companies, decentralized state agencies (such as the offices that allocate funds), nursing homes, hospitals, municipal authorities, welfare providers, housing associations and so forth. Commercial providers have been allowed to enter the supply side of elderly care, making the overall nature of supply more hybrid in nature.

These developments have resulted in major tensions within the system (Breedveld 2003). The public control and guarantee of elderly care facilities are opposed to market competition between service-providing organizations. The relationships between them are partly based on co-operation, both incidental and more permanent, as links of a chain of services; partly, they are based on competition. The drive for greater efficiency leads to an increasing rationalization of activities, deconstructing elderly care provision and organizing it into a set of carefully defined activities.

Dutch elderly care is increasingly about smart networks with a temporary character. Management of elderly care provision is mostly a strategy of leaving room for co-production. Successful elderly care managers have been found to be pragmatic, open and interactive, and intellectual, analytic and with an overview of the wider elderly care sector, rather than only their individual care organization (based on Brandsen and van Hout 2004; van Hout 2006).

THE ORGANIZATIONAL EFFECTS OF CO-MANAGEMENT

As we will argue in this paragraph, the three types of tensions are alleviated by adaptations within the internal organization of service providers. As we have argued, these are basically network tensions that are drawn inward. By implication, efforts to resolve them and restore the cohesion of the organization also encourage network integration. We will discuss these efforts in relation to skills, staffing, structure and management style. These are the organizational aspects in which we have witnessed the most profound changes in our case studies. We will not suggest that they occur within all organizations, nor with the same intensity everywhere, so they must be regarded as potential directions for future development. Systematic research will have to show the exact conditions under which these developments materialize.

A growing need for soft skills

Handling an increasingly ambiguous, but also increasingly significant external environment requires specific skills. One crucial condition for survival is the ability to be pragmatic. When demands are multiple and often contradictory, it pays not to have fierce (political) principles on the nature of the service. For example, it may mean having to treat clients differently. It also requires the ability to think strategically, as contacts with other organizations extend across all levels of the internal organization. Finally, and this is the most far-reaching change, there is the need to invest in 'soft skills'.

To start with, there need to be good lines of communication into those providing new services and those offering the traditional range of services – regardless of whether the two are in one organization. Even if the new service is provided by a unit of the same organization, the work of the various units must be sufficiently integrated. Again, this is the classic tension between differentiation and integration, but one that is clearly made more urgent by diversification. What will also increasingly happen is that staff members operate on the fringes of the traditional organization, communicating either with other units or other organizations. They will need to deal with the uncertainties that accompany joint and spread-out products. The significance of boundary-spanning individuals is likely to increase.

All in all, co-management leads to a demand for the generic skills of people who appreciate the importance of the context within which they work, with an ability to track the changing environment, analyse it and respond. Skills of communication are central. A willingness to work at uncertainties and to cope with ambiguity is important, whatever particular specialist skills are also needed. For many organizations these matters imply a considerable shift in culture, brought about by training and, more importantly, by example.

From staffing to sourcing

What the required skills demand in terms of staffing is difficult to say generally, or without treading on toes. Many third-sector organizations deliver public services with a relational and/or professional character. They therefore depend strongly on people as their most valuable resource: teachers, attendants, nurses, doctors and so forth; professionals and volunteers, staff at the 'frontline' as well as their managers. Any solution to the previously described tensions, such as the acquisition of new skills, is therefore very likely to involve changes at the level of staffing. Although it is often possible to retrain people and coach them, it may not be possible to achieve the desired cultural turn without some individual sacrifices. In this respect, we will note two trends that have emerged from our research.

One important trend we have observed is that formerly long-term relationships between staff and organization are exchanged for more transitory, contract-based relationships. As demand becomes more volatile, numeric, quantitative flexibility becomes necessary in order to adapt to demand-driven changes within the context of (quasi-)markets. Simultaneously, temporary staffing helps to guarantee the continuity of public service delivery and to cope with peak moments in demand. However, when services have a strong relational character (which is especially the case in health care and social services) such temporary arrangements can be at odds with the perceived quality of the services.

In addition to this somewhat predictable movement towards flexibility, we have observed a shift from 'staffing' to 'sourcing'. One can distinguish four types of sourcing:

(1) The combined sourcing of organizations delivering comparable services like home care and elderly care on the basis of flexible contracts and informal, personal networks of contractors and subcontractors (so-called '*ad-sourcing*').
(2) Where the interdependency in public service delivery by third-sector organizations is very strong, we observe temporary project organizations, staffed by employees from several organizations (as in PPP-constructions), in which municipalities, care providers, the police force, housing corporations, project developers, building firms, hospitals, social assistance and voluntary organizations together establish temporary organizations ('*co-sourcing*').
(3) A third and rapidly growing form of sourcing is the one in which specialized staffing agencies deliver staff on a regular basis and actually take over their contracts (traditionally called '*out-sourcing*').
(4) The last form covers the mergers of third-sector organizations to increase their labour potential ('*in-sourcing*').

A growing divide between formal and informal structure

All developments lead to a diminishing significance of formal structure. As the pressure for accountability grows, organizations start to decouple formal requirements from actual activities (cf. Meyer and Rowan 1992). Many new activities are initially introduced within separate functional units. The question, in terms of structure, is whether those separate units should be integrated with other functions. Yet as the activities of service providers diversify, the need to maintain legal and administrative barriers will grow. For a start, external supervisors will demand clear demarcations when public funds are used. For example, housing grants awarded to schemes for the elderly are expected not to spill over into elderly care, even when housing and care are offered as a single package and when they are in practice inseparable. In addition, reducing the financial risks involved in new activities makes it sensible to restrain formal integration, even when in practice old and new activities increasingly blend into one another.

Actual practice always differs from the blueprints, but the combination of developments described above will widen the gap. The need for compensating mechanisms of integration will grow accordingly. Maintaining organizational coherence will increasingly rely on informal rather than formal mechanisms. A greater distinction between the formal and informal structure is therefore likely. If it is to achieve effective co-ordination, the organization will have to take on more characteristics of the 'missionary' type (cf. Mintzberg *et al.* 2003 [1991]: 224).

From contracting and hierarchy to trust and persuasion

This, in turn, fits well with the rising significance of external relations. When specialist skills and information are needed, but they are not available within the organizations themselves, members must look to their network to access them. In addition, the need for additional financial resources and partners requires a visible presence in local and regional networks, if not a role in local governance. Given such requirements, the identification of interesting new partners will be a skill of increasing value, both at the management and the street level. One difficulty is to assess the reliability of other organizations as future partners. Here we come back to the tension between competition and co-operation. On the one hand, the integration of local and regional networks requires an investment in long-term, trust-based relationships, with a select group of partners. On the other hand, greater emphasis on competition and contracting upsets the stability of at least some of these relationships, as already noted in research on the quasi-markets established during the 1980s and 1990s (e.g. Bartlett *et al.* 1998). When an organization has a strong internal culture of co-operation, as we argued for in the previous section, it therefore makes sense to export that culture to its relationships with stakeholders, rather than to focus on hard contracting.

As the organization's core tasks are increasingly fulfilled in partnerships, they shift outward, and the organization's boundaries become more fluid. By implication, it may increasingly become a network-like organization. One should not get carried away by such a concept: local service deliverers are not international businesses competing on dynamic global markets and one should be wary of using fashionable concepts where they do not apply. Nevertheless, some of the looseness of external networks will be drawn inward and this may require a change of management style. As managers no longer maintain full control of the services their organization offers, they increasingly have to operate through incentives and persuasion rather than hierarchy. This is where co-management starts to undermine the managerialist ethic: managers will lose power as their organizations diversify and stretch out. To be more precise, they will have to exercise a different kind of power, with an emphasis on charisma and inspiration rather than rule-making. Also, it will become more important to watch the quality of the organization's gatekeepers and boundary spanners. There is a potential trade-off between effective gate-keeping and responsiveness to network partners, although this is not necessarily the case.

Case 2: Housing association diversification

In 2004–5 Tilburg University (The Netherlands) and Coventry University (UK) conducted a joint research project into the diversification of the activities of social landlords in Ireland, Italy, The Netherlands and the UK (Brandsen *et al.* 2006). Most of the landlords provide some additional personal services to residents in need, whether health and personal care for the elderly, care for those with learning difficulties and other disabilities, the provision of welfare benefits advice and debt counselling or capacity building for residents looking for work or wanting new skills. Practice varies between associations. Some undertake these tasks themselves, while others work with specialist partners to deliver such services on a contractual basis. For instance, some employ nurses for elderly care directly, whereas other organizations do so indirectly by entering into an alliance with health-care providers. Some landlords provide services only to their own tenants, whereas others also offer them to local people who are not their tenants, but who are residents of the same neighbourhood and/or members of the same community.

These new activities have required landlords to rethink their staff policy, their internal communication and their criteria for adopting new initiatives. When should they say no? On a more fundamental level, it has raised questions about their organizational mission. Is their purpose to provide social rented housing, as a goal, or is social rented housing their means of solving problems in neighbourhoods, as a means?

CONCLUSION

Co-management brings third-sector organizations into the public services, and into an environment that has been subject to extensive changes. As a result, the organizations are pulled towards differentiation, while they simultaneously take initiatives that encourage integration. This manifests itself in (at least) three ways. In relations with partners within their networks, providers find that they must both compete and co-operate, trust and distrust. The requirements for accountability increase, each of them reasonable in itself, but a threat to the organization's integrity when they come together in complex and contradictory configurations. Diversification appears to be a way of integrating activities that are artificially differentiated, but it may threaten the organization's core business.

The third-sector organizations we observed found various ways to ease the tensions: flexible staffing arrangements, the acquirement of new skills, decoupling and a different style of management. Given that we only conducted a limited number of case studies, it is too early to assess the general implications of what we have observed. These are potential directions in which similar organizations could develop. If future research were to reproduce the same findings on a more systematic basis, it would be evidence of a powerful innovative force in the contemporary welfare state.

NOTE

1 Hybridity, in our definition, refers to a mix of co-ordinating mechanisms. 'Pure' state, market and third-sector organizations rarely exist, so this must be regarded as a movement along a continuum away from idealtypical representations. Hybridity represents the stage where elements from different idealtypes become entangled to the point where there is no longer a clear match with any single type.

REFERENCES

Ashkenas, R., Ulrich, D., Jick, T. and Kerr, S. (2002) *The Boundaryless Organization*, San Francisco, CA: Jossey-Bass.

Bartlett, W., Roberts, J. A. and Le Grand, J. (1998) 'The Development of Quasi-Markets in the 1990s' in J. A. Roberts, J. Le Grand and W. Bartlett (eds) *A Revolution in Social Policy: Quasi-Market Reforms in the 1990s*. Bristol: The Policy Press.

Brandsen, T. and van Hout, E. (2004) Public Management Dilemmas in Dutch Domiciliary Care. Paper presented at the Eighth International Research Symposium on Public Management, Budapest, 31 March – 2 April.

Brandsen, T., Cardoso Ribeiro, T. and Farnell, R. (2006) *Housing Association Diversification in Europe*, Coventry: The Rex Group. Available at www.uvt.nl/kameleon/rexreport.pdf.

Brandsen, T., van de Donk, W. and Putters, K. (2005) Griffins or Chameleons? Hybridity as a Permanent and Inevitable Characteristic of the Third Sector, *International Journal of Public Administration*. 28: 9–10 pp749–65.

Breedveld, E. (2003) *Thuiszorg in Bedrijf: Herstructurering van de Thuiszorgbranche tussen 1987 en 1997*, Tilburg: Van Spaendonck.

De Bruijn, H., ten Heuvelhof, E. and In 't Veld, R. (2002) *Process Management*, Dordrecht: Kluwer Academic.

Jaffee, D. (2001) *Organization Theory: Tension and Change*, New York: McGraw-Hill.

Kenis, P. (2006) 'Hybriditeit Vanuit een Netwerktheoretisch Perspectief' in T. Brandsen, W. van de Donk and P. Kenis (eds) *Meervoudig Bestuur: Publieke Dienstverlening door Hybride Organisaties*. The Hague: Lemma.

Klijn, E. H. (1996) Analyzing and Managing Policy Processes in Complex Networks, *Administration and Society*. 28: 1 pp90–119.

Klijn, E. H., Koppenjan, J. F. M. and Termeer, C. J. A. M. (1995) Managing Networks in the Public Sector, *Public Administration*. 73: 3 pp437–54.

Koppenjan, J. and Klijn, E. H. (2004) *Managing Uncertainties in Networks: A Network Approach to Problem Solving and Decision Making*, London: Routledge.

Lawrence, P. R. and Lorsch, J. W. (1967) *Organization and Environment: Managing Differentiation and Integration*, Homewood, IL: Irwin.

Meyer, J. W. and Rowan, B. (1992) 'Institutionalised Organisations: Formal Structure as Myth and Ceremony' in J. W. Meyer and W. R. Scott (eds) *Organizational Environments: Ritual and Rationality*. London: Sage.

Mintzberg, H., Lampel, J., Quinn, J. B. and Ghoshal, S. (2003 [1991]) *The Strategy Process: Concepts, Contexts, Cases*, Upper Saddle River, NJ: Pearson Education.

Pfeffer, J. and Salancik, G. R. (1978) *The External Control of Organizations: A Resource Dependence Perspective*, New York: Harper & Row.

Power, M. (1997) *The Audit Society: Rituals of Verification*, Oxford: Oxford University Press.

Van Hout, E. J. T. (2006) 'Hybriditeit in de Ouderenzorg: Leidraad voor Innovatie' in T. Brandsen, W. van de Donk and P. Kenis (eds) *Meervoudig Bestuur: Publieke Dienstverlening door Hybride Organisaties*. The Hague: Lemma.

CO-GOVERNANCE WITHIN NETWORKS AND THE NON-PROFIT – FOR-PROFIT DIVIDE

A cross-cultural perspective on the evolution of domiciliary elderly care

Ingo Bode

INTRODUCTION

Recently, there has been remarkable change in (publicly managed) social welfare across the western world. One of its triggers was the introduction of *market regulations* following the 'New Public Management' doctrine, with its 'explicit standards of performance, [. . .] emphasis on output control, increased competition; contracts (and) devolution' (Christensen and Laegreid 2002: 19). At the same time, however, the contemporary governance literature stresses an increasingly participatory role of '*third-sector*' organizations, with 'co-governance' becoming an innovative way to organize public services (Kooiman 2003: 96–114). This mode of governance is supposedly based on *networks*, understood as inter-organizational arrangements superseding both a hierarchical approach to welfare provision and the (early) simplistic concepts of the New Public Management gurus (Hudson 2004; Radcliffe and Dent 2005; Tenbensel 2005). Networks are supplanting state-bureaucratic and 'pure' market governance, so the story goes.

Elderly care is an organizational field where one can easily test out whether this narrative tells us the full truth about the actual dynamics of change. While marketization has gone relatively far here over the last years, partnerships between statutory and non-statutory actors are widespread as well (Ascoli and Ranci 2002). At the same time, the overall evolution of social care systems is highly influenced by *cultural traditions* shaping both quasi-market regulations and partnerships (within networks).

Against this background, this study undertakes a comparison of elderly care networks under conditions of marketization in different (national) contexts. It basically aims at testing the previously mentioned 'network narrative'. With a focus on *domiciliary provision* which is commonly deemed an expanding domain and which involves the lion's share of the frail elderly, the analysis will embrace three different jurisdictions: Germany, France and England. These countries represent two European worlds of 'welfare capitalism' – the liberal and the corporatist one – although it will become obvious that this distinction does not tell us the full story about international variation. The following argument is based on an explorative, albeit empirically substantiated, investigation on how networks for elderly care (have) develop(ed), especially as regards co-governance, which is understood here as consensual regulation shared by public, civic and professional actors. The next section briefly elaborates on the concepts of network and co-governance. In the second section, developments in home care across the three countries are pictured. The final part provides a comparative assessment and presents theoretical conclusions with respect to both the co-governance theme and what is labelled here the non-profit–for-profit divide in social care systems.

NETWORKS AND CO-GOVERNANCE IN THE SOCIAL (CARE) SECTOR

Over the last decades, the notion of the 'network' has made its way as a catch-all category for characterizing social and organizational change. As Hudson (2004: 78) puts it, 'the network theme has become ubiquitous, though fragmented among disciplines, theoretical bases, levels of analysis and substantive foci of research.' From a particular perspective, networks are dealt with in the debate on partnerships in social care systems (see, for example, Powell and Exworthy 2002). These systems are, by tradition, composed of several elements that all contribute to the process of service delivery. To understand their complex nature, it helps to distinguish different elements, which are referred to as fundamental in the literature on social service provision.

First of all, social care systems have in most western countries come under the control of *welfare bureaucracies* (Anttonen *et al.* 2003). These bureaucracies constitute a 'substantive ethical domain' (du Gay 2000: 2) in which standards of resource allocation are based on normative grounds (such as social merit or human rights) and applied with a consideration of individual situations. Moreover, social care is influenced by norms of *welfare professionalism* (Harrison and Smith 2004). Professionalism implies particular social orientations, which may overlap with the ones held by welfare bureaucrats but, analytically, are independent from them. Ideally, professionalism is based on the application of scientific knowledge in the light of unique cases, with practical judgements formed during real-life encounters, irrespective of any other motivational background (Freidson 2001).

Furthermore, the social care sector is in many countries entangled with organizations that follow particular values or needs rather than aims of profit making or of complying with hierarchical norms. Indeed, the provision of social services is at the core of what is commonly labelled the *third sector* (Anheier and Seibel 1990; Evers and Laville 2004). To be sure, non-profit organizations comprise a number of different orientations and practices, and many of them operate as 'multi-purpose' organizations (Hasenfeld and Gidron 2005) or penetrate the mainstream economy in order to meet particular social ends (Bode *et al.* 2006). In that sense, they are hybrids (Brandsen *et al.* 2005). However, the genuine distinctiveness of these organizations resides in their associational foundations. Ideally, voluntary organizations exist as groups of citizens committed to a mutually agreed collective purpose which, very often, concerns the welfare of a larger community or the proliferation of ideas on *which kind* of welfare shall be given prevalence or on *how* to provide it. These orientations often extend from the voluntary members to professional staff (Bode 2004) and may be termed *civic orientations*, as they frequently address deliberations within the political system. There are plenty of historical examples of non-profit organizations participating in social welfare provision in that sense (Evers 1993; Bode 2006a).

Given this multi-tiered structure of social care systems, it is highly plausible that these systems take shape as *networks* of actors and organizations. While studies on social welfare provision have sometimes paid attention to this, the network theme has been given much more attention in a second body of literature addressing inter-firm relations within competitive environments (Borgatti and Foster 2003). Networks are understood here as a 'distinct form of coordinating economic activity' (Powell 1990: 301) which contrasts with markets and hierarchies. The analytical emphasis lies upon the interplay of strategic actors who are interested in their own well-being, but understand that they may perform better by going for partnerships centring around product development, joint marketing or common research. One reason for the growth of these networks is a high task complexity implying the integration of diverse specialists. This is conducive to long-term and reiterated exchanges creating interdependency, reciprocal lines of communication, as well as shared values, norms and beliefs (DiMaggio and Powell 1983).

From this discussion, one may derive the idea that the diverse (groups of) actors involved in social service provision will engage in networking even within competitive environments. This especially makes sense in the context of emerging social care markets. However, it appears questionable whether networks overcome self-interest at any time and in any respect. Rather, one may assume that, as Davies (2005: 312) puts it, 'market transactions are a form of networking' so that networks, including in social care, are composed of a particular *variety of cognitive orientations*, that is, welfare-bureaucratic, professional, civic *and* competition-driven (market) orientations. The analysis of networks in the (social) care sector can considerably benefit from taking this multitude of orientations and their interplay into account, as will be shown in the following sections.

Yet one should make a distinction between *two (sets of) rationales* pervading these networks. The *first rationale* comprises bureaucratic, professional and civic orientations focusing on a particular idea of priorities in social welfare provision. Basically, this idea consists of taking (perceived) individual needs as a starting point in order to seek 'case-sensitive' solutions to meet these needs. A major hypothesis of this study is that welfare professionalism, throughout the second half of the last century, spread into the public *and* – to the extent that it became involved into social service provision – into the voluntary sector. A further hypothesis is that civic agencies have confronted the public sector with their particular orientations while public authorities often engaged in formal co-operation with the former. The result was a (more or less fuzzy) 'domain consensus' on how to develop social care (Hudson 2004: 83–6). In other terms, there were more or less deeply entrenched routines of co-governance.

However, and this is a final hypothesis underlying the argument of this study, the consensus has been (further) complicated through the proliferation of profit-oriented orientations within social care systems, fuelled by a fight for survival in competitive markets and by micro-economic management doctrines flourishing in such an environment. These orientations appear as a *second rationale* in those social care networks that have taken shape over the last ten or fifteen years.

While problems of inter-agency, or inter-professional, co-ordination have been extensively dealt with by the literature on social care (e.g. Lewis 2002; Leichsenring 2004; Brown and Cullis 2006), few scholars have thus far looked at what happens to partnerships in social (or, in our case, elderly) care when these two rationales face each other within networks, or, in other terms, when marketization meets national traditions of 'consensus building'. Especially, one should examine the particular character that co-governance adopts in marketized networks of organized care, as well as the evolving role of third-sector organizations within them.

DOMICILIARY ELDERLY CARE IN THREE COUNTRIES, PAST AND PRESENT

Domiciliary care embraces different forms of services, ranging from out-patient medical care over nursing to housekeeping work. Internationally, the frontiers between these different pillars are not clear-cut, neither in everyday practice nor in the institutional design of care systems. In the following, systematic distinctions between different kinds of home care will be avoided. It will be emphasized that, irrespective of international variations, home care proceeds by the consecutive or parallel actions of organizations that are linked to each other in one way or another. Thus, social care is provided though *networks*. One may also consider the involved individuals (especially relatives) or public interest groups (e.g. pensioner organizations) as being part of this network. Yet their enrolment is located at a level different from the process of 'organized' care, which is the focus of what follows.

A key point of interest is the evolution of such networks with recent institutional change. This change proceeds on the grounds of different 'cultural foundations' (Pfau-Effinger 2005: 25) and can be expected to vary internationally in a number of ways. The following sections describe developments in Germany, France and Britain. They draw on evidence from the wider literature, on the one hand, and a range of case studies and interviews with experts, on the other hand (a full list of these sources cannot be provided here, but see Bode 2006a and 2006b). It will be sketched where and how the 'domain consensus' in pre-market home care provision took shape and which patterns of network relations and co-governance have emerged with marketization.

Germany

The *German* elderly care system is ambiguous in being relatively wide-ranging in terms of coverage and institutional organization, on the one hand, but fragmented and under high economic pressure, on the other hand (see Kondratowitz *et al.* 2002; Evers and Sachße 2003; Roth and Reichert 2004). Historically, there is a well-entrenched division of labour between the state and (federated) voluntary agencies which, as early as the 1920s, became eligible for public subsidies provided they were willing to run social services. The so-called 'welfare associations' (*Wohlfahrtsverbände*) thus turned out to be important players in German home care networks – a configuration often referred to as 'social corporatism'.

Especially in the period following World War II, the state was promoting welfare professionalism. Yet as the voluntary sector developed its infrastructure (e.g. universities of applied sciences or professional associations) it became a source of professionalism on its own. In parallel, these associations maintained their role as community organizations. Under their roof, many 'lay' people were running activities such as socializing or offering practical support in everyday life. From the late 1970s onwards, in a number of regions, non-profit organizations received a remit from public bodies to develop 'care centres' (*Sozialstationen*), conceived of as multi-service agencies providing various kinds of professional care with complementary, informal inputs from volunteers. A key idea behind this policy was that the 'care centres' should be the gatekeepers to a great variety of services. The welfare associations entrusted with this role preserved a large measure of autonomy in running their services. Home care provision was far from comprehensive at the time. Yet there was a clear impulse towards a broader coverage of needs for home care. By the end of the 1980s, the centres were entitled to additional resources paid out of the public health care insurance budget. This was when the 'domain consensus' in German home care networks reached its peak.

In 1996, a long-term care insurance scheme was established, together with a *quasi-market regulation* for domiciliary elderly care. The administrative bodies of the insurance (which are independent subunits of the quasi-public health care funds) conduct the assessment of claimants and are supposed to provide the latter with basic information on care facilities (although they rarely manage to do so). Beneficiaries may contact a municipal advice centre, but in many places there is no sound system of counselling. Users can opt for a cash option through which they receive a monthly allowance, used to recompense private providers of care. Otherwise they are entitled, through kind of a voucher, to a package of services the provider of which they choose from a range of agencies with different labels (for-profit, faith-based, non-profit). Care providers compete for clients who are reimbursed by the insurance for a limited number of service hours and who may privately purchase additional services. In the first years after the long-term care insurance was established, domiciliary care provision was markedly expanding. However, the insurance's budgets have recently been decreasing as measured per frail elderly person. Also, the managers of the insurance funds seek to set tight time-frames on scrupulously defined modules of care when they negotiate over fees for services with associations of providers.

The pressure on prices (as reimbursed by the insurance) has led to a partial de-professionalization in the sector and to a more Tayloristic organization of labour. Quality issues are mainly handled through a wide-meshed system of external (quasi-public) control. Non-profit organizations active in the home care system have to cope with market conditions which reward time saving and dispassionate service delivery. This also applies to for-profit agencies, which are mostly small businesses set up by professionals with a former career in public or non-profit organizations. This may be why for-profit entrepreneurs have in some places adjusted their practices to what traditional non-profit providers consider to be their special assets, for instance, the organization of spiritual support. Having said that, faith-based non-profit agencies try hard to bring their traditional reputation to bear, arguing that it is their very tradition that makes them trustworthy providers. It has, however, become more difficult for them to involve volunteers to complement their professional services, which means that one of their competitive advantages is endangered. Thus, while marketization is embedded in the pre-market 'system culture', it does have an impact.

It especially affects the *network relations* in the home care system. On the one hand, numerous non-profit providers have tried to build alliances in order to achieve economics of scale without lowering quality standards. As they are often on good terms with local hospitals, they seek to develop a service chain from hospital treatment through home care to complementary services. On the other hand, many providers are reluctant to collaborate with other elements of the care system, as this may be viewed a waste of precious time or a helping hand to competitors. Case management is poorly developed since a sound system of referrals is missing. There are difficulties in establishing gate-keepers who can gather reliable information about available providers. Also, the mutual adjustment between nursing on the one hand, and personal care or complementary services on the other hand, is by many considered insufficient. Complementary services are organized separately either by isolated voluntary agencies or by small businesses, without any particular stake in elderly care.

As regards *co-governance*, local and national round tables are held where representatives of public authorities and providers discuss (but do not settle on) infrastructural issues. In everyday practice, there is no focal organization deciding on the development of services. Public bodies barely feel accountable for the co-ordination of the overall infrastructure, let alone the supervision of those parts of the home care system not covered by long-term care insurance. It is true that they face a never-ending debate over quality issues, as well as pressure to improve what is often regarded as a cold-blooded service industry. The umbrella organizations of the providers (including the commercial ones) are vigorously lobbying for regulations that impose new quality standards on providers and purchasers. Having said that, there appear to be clear limits to the establishment of co-operative networks in the current German home care system.

France

Studies in the development of elderly care in *France* also point at both creeping institutionalization and a fragmented organization of domiciliary provision (Frossard *et al.* 2004; Cour des Comptes 2005; Rivard 2006). Historically, there was a clearer separation between the state and voluntary agencies than in Germany. However, a good deal of social service provision remained under the responsibility of publicly subsidized non-profit agencies, including care for the elderly. Voluntary organizations became deeply involved in the provision of personal care (*aide ménagaire*), while paramedical help was (and continues to be) provided by independent or municipal nurses and funded by national health insurance.

Some associations providing personal care set up care facilities during the 1950s, with the help of volunteers living in their neighbourhood. As a consequence, they became eligible for funds from public bodies and social insurance. With a licence from their county's authority, voluntary agencies provided a number of service hours mainly to users with lower incomes. In some places, municipalities founded their own agencies, but very often concluded agreements with voluntary organizations mandated to deliver basic domiciliary services. Patterns of 'local corporatism' developed, that is, symbiotic relationships between public and voluntary agencies based on agreements between notables and local politicians. Over the following decades, personal care providers tended to strengthen the role of paid staff and to concentrate the participation of volunteers on administrative functions. This was also because the number of available volunteers was decreasing. Some of them created integrated service centres offering both nursing and personal care, a model also used by municipal providers. Although the service infrastructure remained patchy and did not fully meet the growing demand, France saw the creeping emergence of co-operative networks based on a local 'domain consensus' between the voluntary sector and public authorities. This consensus also embraced the issue of professionalization. At the national level, non-profit providers (and their umbrella organizations) were lobbying for new training policies and higher salaries in the personal care sector. The state introduced new diplomas and offered to reimburse providers for increased wages.

From the 1990s onwards, however, public policies have also encouraged the employment of unskilled care workers in private households through generous exemptions from taxes and pay-roll contributions to social security. While nursing remains highly regulated, personal care has become increasingly based on case-by-case recruitments. In this way, a *market rationale* was introduced into the sector. Personal care providers were now competing with organizations leasing private employees to frail elderly people, with regional social service departments tending to opt arbitrarily for case-by-case employment instead of for professional services.

This has slightly changed with the establishment of a long-term care benefit scheme in 2002. The social service departments of the counties now grant every frail elderly person an earmarked allowance which is meant to cover all required services. This is based on an assessment of need and premised on the condition that the person's state of health exhibits a certain degree of frailty. High-income earners have to pay user fees. However, the Government recently launched a plan encouraging the commercial provision of personal care services. Providers and counties may now opt out of the funding regime based on administered prices, with intensified competition as a result. The home care market is also supposed to be fuelled by a scheme through which employers may grant pre-funded vouchers to their workers. Though the involvement of private firms has thus far remained an exception, things may change in the near future. The tendency towards more market governance persists, as does the separation between nursing and personal care.

Today, two developments can be singled out which have notable impacts on the *network relations* materializing in the French home care sector. First, while the involvement of personal care providers often still remains embedded in pre-existing partnerships, there is evidence that some counties have chosen open competition between providers. Against this background, non-profit providers invest much energy in the marketing of their services. They address new target groups (people with higher incomes) and take into account that reimbursed care services do not cover the full range of existing needs. Many agencies are seeking to conquer new market segments through the opening of 'service shops' and through nationally operating call-centres which direct advice-seeking clients to service providers belonging to 'associational alliances'. These investments are realized through joint ventures with banks and insurance companies looking for cross-selling opportunities. As a result of all this, organizational energies are withdrawn from vertical or horizontal co-operation within the care system.

Second, there are new developments in *co-governance*. In reaction to the rise of private care employees, the umbrella organizations of the non-profit providers had developed concepts for the further professionalization of elderly care and run campaigns for new statutory regulations, including earmarked entitlements. Their voice was heard to some extent. The care allowance scheme introduced in 2002 privileges professional services over case-by-case employment and the latter has decreased in numbers. Also, the gate-keeper role of the previously mentioned integrated service centres is strengthened through the injection of additional public money, which is used for employing additional qualified staff. In a number of regions, moreover, new lead-agencies have been created that deal with infrastructural issues, providing counselling and involving voluntary organizations in their management. Sometimes, these agencies are also responsible for needs assessments. Although there still is concern over insufficient co-ordination between the different elements of the elderly care system, now the driving vision is to generalize a strategy of multi-stakeholder governance. These are new impulses for networking that go beyond market governance.

England

The post-war social (care) sector in *England* (that differs in a number of ways from other parts of the UK) is shaped by the central role of public authorities. However, in social services, although the public and voluntary sectors have remained weakly coupled, patterns of consensual co-operation did emerge in many places. Some scholars have even labelled this a 'dual system' (Taylor 2002: 80) based on co-governance and negotiated public policies.

This configuration also emerged in the course of the history of domiciliary care (see Means *et al.* 2002; Baldock 2003: 123–31; Comas-Herera *et al.* 2004; Netten *et al.* 2005). The responsibility for providing care services was devolved to Local Authorities in the late 1960s. Home care then consisted of nursing, guaranteed by the local NHS, and (some) personal care organized by Local Authorities (mainly for low-income earners). Whereas numerous Local Authorities had their own in-house providers, a good deal of personal care was provided by publicly funded voluntary agencies. At this stage, welfare professionalism became part of the corporate identity of Social Service Departments, yet it also set the frame of action for the voluntary agencies involved. On the whole, the voluntary sector remained committed to lay action until the early 1990s and its major mission was to engage publicly with care policies, including quality issues. Due to the priorities of Local Authorities (which had a preference for residential services), the home care supply was in many places insufficiently comprehensive during the first decades of the post-war period. Yet a fuzzy 'domain consensus' existed that nursing and basic personal care services were to be funded by general taxation and kept under the control of public gate-keepers, with the voluntary sector involved as a 'junior partner'. One can say, then, that a public-sector-led system of co-operation existed up to the 1980s.

With the 'Community Care Act' enacted in 1990, large parts of the service field were devolved to independent providers, with only a minor proportion coming from the voluntary sector. Public bodies remained responsible for service supply, in so far as they were to purchase domiciliary care packages on behalf of eligible users. A *fully fledged quasi-market* emerged, with public authorities inviting for tenders and case managers purchasing selected bits of services. Although actual contract policies vary across localities, previous partnerships between public and non-public actors have in the meanwhile often been superseded by quasi-commercial relations. Voluntary agencies involved in the contract business sometimes face harsh shifts in their service portfolios. For many of them, managerial skills and micro-economic excellence have become a priority. By contrast, volunteers turn out to be a more precarious asset as many are reluctant to support frail elderly people in their homes.

The market rationale also applies to public agencies responsible for the management of the care system. Public-sector managers who do not respect given benchmarks (e.g. a certain number of frail people being referred from hospitals to home care services) may be economically 'punished' by their hierarchy. Welfare professionalism has come under attack. This affects not only public case managers, but also numerous suppliers, given that the bulk of services have gone over to independent providers employing rather low-skilled staff while the remit of the NHS has increasingly been confined to very basic nursing. Moreover, user fees have risen markedly. The hours of personal care services funded by local authorities have tripled, but the number of households receiving home care has diminished. An increasing number of the frail elderly depend on an unregulated care market.

As for *network relations*, horizontal and vertical co-ordination between the parties involved in home care is generally poor. Although infrastructural issues are dealt with by 'Local Strategic Partnership Boards' and at occasional meetings between Local Authority managers and representatives of providers, the formal relations between purchaser and providers do barely go beyond the mere business of contracting. Also, there are few (e.g. associational) links between home care providers and the hospital sector (like in Germany). While mergers are widespread, inter-agency co-operation remains exceptional.

However, the voluntary sector has not given up its mission of prioritizing social needs over economic concerns. Although involved in a more business-like service delivery, its contribution to *co-governance* is most vigorous in its role of lobbying for better market regulation. Its expertise has probably contributed to the fact that the quality issue has invaded the social policy agenda in recent years. Since 2004, all personal care providers have been inspected by and have received advice from a national quango. Furthermore, there are efforts to establish comprehensive case management for those receiving publicly funded care. Likewise, single assessment procedures have been introduced. To this, add the meetings of the previously mentioned 'Partnership Boards', which allow the voices of several stakeholders to be heard at least to some extent. There is still more to English home care networks than mere market governance.

CHANGING NETWORKS, CHANGING CO-GOVERNANCE

This succinct review of evolutions in the home care sectors of Germany, France and England provides us with a number of basic insights. First of all, compared to what has become a widespread understanding in the literature on inter-firm relations in the mainstream economy – which are thought to evolve towards more collaborative action – the elderly care sector has developed in the opposite direction. In this field, networks preceded market relations. The provision of care services was never a monopoly of the public sector, but was more or less shared with the 'third sector', through reiterated exchanges creating interdependency, and through mutual adjustment rather than hierarchical governance or market competition. Notwithstanding the latent (and still existing) strains between professions or between different layers of the care system, there was a *propensity* to stick to a 'domain consensus' that embraces the rationales of welfare bureaucracies, professionalism and civic action.

The new thing about networks in home care is, from the 1990s onwards, the *invasion of the market rationale* into pre-existing networks. Elderly care systems nowadays comprise, at various levels, management strategies stressing a 'for-profit'-orientation, in the sense of maximizing measurable outputs per invested (monetary) input. A *new for-profit – non-profit divide* has emerged as a result. Thus, the evolution of these systems, irrespective of national particularities, is indicative of a *transformation* of networks rather than of an overall tendency from hierarchical (or market) governance to network governance.

This transformation is complex in nature, though. According to the 'network narrative' developed in the organizational studies literature, marketization does not exclude inter-organizational collaboration. To an extent, this assertion is confirmed by the evidence. Besides mergers and efforts to build service chains (mainly in Germany), there is collaboration between competing agencies in fields like lobbying for or the negotiation of market regulations. Yet the considerable task complexity, and the high importance of (inter-)professional work in the sector, do not imply more encompassing and cordial inter-agency exchange.

Rather, in all countries under study, the flourishing 'business culture' has set new limits to *welfare professionalism*, though the latter continues to have an impact, as shown by successful initiatives strengthening quality inspection and case management. Moreover, *welfare bureaucracies* have partially resigned from the 'domain consensus' as public managers increasingly arrange their relation with providers according to a (quasi-) for-profit rationale. To be sure, standardized resource allocation based on normative rules persists – yet public managers appear less concerned with verifying whether these rules are applied in due consideration of individual circumstances. As regards *civic orientations*, it is obvious that voluntary agencies now 'go market', as they are deploying much energy for developing business tools and for winning new customers. This, in all probability, proceeds at the expense of the cultivation of their associational foundations including the involvement of volunteers – with the latter becoming ever more difficult given the erosion of traditional patterns of lay action in the social care sector.

Having said that, *co-governance* – which is defined here as consensual regulation shared by public, civic and professional actors – persists, though less vigorously. Third-sector organizations still participate in 'domain consensus' building, e.g. in Germany where the conditions of service provision are partially subject to collective bargaining and where round tables provide for mutual adjustment when it comes to the deliberation of quality standards. Similar efforts occur in France where provider associations are involved in discussions about how further to professionalize the sector. Moreover, third-sector organizations still translate perceived needs into political action, particularly in England. They transcend market forces by having their civic voice heard in the public sphere. However, this increasingly proceeds through the agency of umbrella structures drawing on the reputation of voluntary organizations as 'common cause' agencies. The agencies' investment in civic action appears to be increasingly decoupled from the everyday 'care business'.

One has to account for *inter-cultural variation*, though. Germany has more or less followed the international tendency towards a more marketized public management of social services (Bönker and Wollmann 2000). However, German post-corporatism appears as a configuration prone to produce new non-profit alliances on the growing quasi-markets. The long-standing tradition of intermediary organizations being granted a quasi-public status provides an avenue to inter-organizational co-ordination both within and between associational pillars. It also leaves some room for institutionalized co-governance to persist. On the other hand, the comparatively strong reliance on individual households as independent (market) actors, as realized in the use of the quasi-'voucher system', goes back to the family-based tradition in the German care sector (see Pfau-Effinger 2005) and paradoxically opens the door to more market-oriented behaviour by the cared-for or their relatives.

In France, the emphasis on public responsibility for social welfare provision exerts a certain pressure to ensure uniform standards under statutory control. As Cole and Jones (2005: 584) rightly argue, 'the ideological underpinnings of the NPM debate do not find a receptive terrain in French public administration.' This is why regulations that *de facto* imply a more competitive provider landscape – such as fiscal advantages for employing staff in private households – have appeared outside any systematic quasi-market agenda. Rather, governments have *simultaneously* sought to establish a more professionalized and (recently) more integrated infrastructure of care services. Also, the strong tradition of 'clientelistic governance' (Gaudin 1998) still favours particularistic local agreements, with uneven patterns of care provision over the French territory as a consequence.

Concerning England, the tradition of British liberalism has clearly favoured the proliferation of market orientations within public governance. However, many have argued that public interventionism has remained vital in spite of being transformed into the steering of contexts (Clarke 2004). While the 'market doctrine' has been firmly established within the English social welfare sector (Beresford 2005), this has recently been accompanied by two other tendencies: a higher esteem for independent and often voluntary-sector-based service providers; and a strong(er) commitment to quality control. A more market-based style of governance then goes along with the tension-led revitalization of two further British traditions: the fostering of public well-being through charitable initiative, and the ambition of the central state to control basic structures of the social care system. The overall result is that co-governance plays a role, but rather as a complement to the steering process, given that everyday business is very much subject to public control and market governance.

Notwithstanding these cultural differences, there is a cross-country transformation of home care networks. While home care networks continue to be based on several overlapping rationales, their architecture is changing from a (quasi-)corporatist framework towards loose coupling under market pressure. The invasion of the market rationale is disorganizing those network relations that were previously based on a (tentative) 'domain consensus'. Accordingly, in our days, co-governance cannot be understood as a mode of co-ordination that supplants hierarchical 'government' or 'pure' market co-ordination. Rather, it has been fundamental to the building of mixed care systems before being exposed to a new non-profit – for-profit divide – and it turns out to be less consistent than in previous times. The overall result is *'nervous' network governance*, fraught with volatility and permanent tensions (see also Bode 2006a). Against this background, it is hard to imagine that, on a larger scale, clients or their relatives are empowered truly to participate in the very *co-production* of care services. Deliberations within the third-sector organizations involved may reflect the concerns of users, which may then be voiced in encounters with public authorities. However, market pressures and the overall weakening of consensus building set clear limits to 'democratic' elderly care.

REFERENCES

Anheier, H. K. and Seibel, W. eds (1990) *The Third Sector: Comparative Studies of Non-Profit-Organisations*, Berlin & New York: De Gruyter.

Anttonen, A., Baldock, J. and Sipilä, J. (2003) 'Patterns of Social Care in Five Industrial Societies: Explaining Diversity' in A. Anttonen, J. Baldock and J. Sipilä (eds) *The Young, the Old and the State: Social Care Systems in Five Industrial Nations*. Cheltenham: Edward Elgar.

Ascoli, U. and Ranci, C. eds (2002) *Dilemmas of the Welfare Mix: The New Structure of Welfare in an Era of Privatisation*, New York: Kluwer Academic/Plenum Publishers.

Baldock, J. (2003) 'Social Care in the United Kingdom: A Pattern of Discretionary Social Administration' in A. Anttonen, J. Baldock and J. Sipilä (eds) *The Young, the Old and the State: Social Care Systems in Five Industrial Nations*. Cheltenham: Edward Elgar.

Beresford, P. (2005) Redistributing Profit and Loss: The New Economics of the Market and Social Welfare, *Critical Social Policy*. 25: 4 pp464 – 82.

Bode, I. (2004) 'The Quality of Nonprofit Employment – Patterns and Dynamics of Work Organisation in the German Third Sector' in C. Stecker and A. Zimmer (eds) *Strategy Mix for Nonprofit Organisations: Vehicles for Social and Labour Market Integration*. New York: Kluwer Adademic/Plenum Press.

—— (2006a) Disorganised Welfare Mixes: Voluntary Agencies and New Governance Regimes in Western Europe, *Journal of European Social Policy*. 19: 4 pp346 – 59.

—— (2006b) New Moral Economies of Welfare: The Case of Domiciliary Elderly Care in Germany, France and Britain, *European Societies*. 8: 4 pp527 – 44.

Bode, I., Evers, A. and Schulz, A. D. (2006) 'Social Enterprises: Can Hybridisation Be Sustainable?' in M. Nyssens (ed.) *Social Enterprises: Between Markets, Public Policies and Community*. London: Routledge.

Bönker, F. and Wollmann, H. (2000) 'The Rise and Fall of a Social Service Regime: Marketisation of German Social Services in Historical Perspective' in H. Wollmann and E. Schroeter (eds) *Comparing Public Sector Reform in Britain and Germany*. Aldershot: Ashgate.

Borgatti, S. P. and Foster, P. G. (2003) The Network Paradigm in Organisational Research: A Review and Typology, *Journal of Management*. 29: 6 pp991 – 1013.

Brandsen, T., van de Donk, W. and Putters, K. (2005) Griffins or Chameleons? Hybridity as a Permanent and Inevitable Characteristic of the Third Sector, *International Journal of Public Administration*. 28: 9 – 10 pp749 – 66.

Brown, L. and Cullis, J. (2006) 'Team Production' and Policy for the Care of Older People: Problems with Theory and Evidence, *Policy Studies*. 27: 1 pp55 – 70.

Christensen, T. and Laegreid, P. (2002) 'A Transformative Perspective on Administrative Reforms' in T. Christensen and P. Laegreid (eds) *New Public Management: The Transformation of Ideas and Practice*. Aldershot: Ashgate.

Clarke, J. (2004) *Changing Welfare, Changing States: New Directions in Social Policy*, London: Sage.

Cole, A. and Jones, G. (2005) Reshaping the State: Administrative Reform and New Public Management in France, *Governance*. 18: 4 pp567 – 88.

Comas-Herrera, A., Wittenberg, R. and Pickard, L. (2004) 'Long-Term Care for Older People in the United Kingdom: Structure and Challenges' in M. Knapp, D. Challis, J. L. Fernández and A. Netten (eds) *Long-Term Care: Matching Resources and Needs*. Aldershot: Ashgate.

Cour des Comptes (2005) *Les personnes âgées dépendantes: rapport au Président de la République Suivi des réponses des administrations et des Organismes Intéressés*, Paris: Journal Officiel.

Davies, J. S. (2005) Local Governance and the Dialectics of Hierarchy, Market and Network, *Policy Studies*. 25: 3/4 pp311 – 35.

DiMaggio, P. J. and Powell, W. W. (1983) The Iron Cage Revisited: Institutional Isomorphism and Collective Rationality in Organisational Fields, *American Sociological Review*. 48: 1 pp147 – 60.

Du Gay, P. (2000) *In Praise of Bureaucracy: Weber – Organisation – Ethics*, London: Sage.

Evers, A. (1993) 'The Welfare Mix Approach: Understanding the Pluralisms of Welfare States' in A. Evers and I. Svetlik (eds) *Balancing Pluralism: New Welfare Mixes in Care for the Elderly*. Aldershot: Avebury.

Evers, A. and Laville, J. L. eds (2004) *The Third Sector in Europe*, Cheltenham: Edward Elgar.

Evers, A. and Sachße, C. (2003) 'Social Care Services for Children and Older People in Germany: Distinct and Separate Histories' in A. Anttonen, J. Baldock and J. Sipilä (eds) *The Young, the Old and the State: Social Care Systems in Five Industrial Nations*. Cheltenham: Edward Elgar.

Freidson, E. (2001) *Professionalism: The Third Logic*, Chicago, IL: University of Chicago Press.

Frossard, M., Genin, N., Guisset, M. J. and Villez, A. (2004) 'Providing Integrated Health and Social Care for Older Persons in France: An Old Idea with a Great Future' in K. Leichsenring and A. Alaszewski (eds) *Providing Integrated Health and Social Care for Older Persons: A European Overview of Issues at Stake*. Aldershot: Ashgate.

Gaudin, J. P. (1998) Modern Governance, Yesterday and Today: Some Clarifications to Be Gained from French Government Policies, *International Social Science*. 55: 1 pp47–55.

Harrison, S. and Smith, C. (2004) Trust and Moral Motivation: Redundant Resources in Health and Social Care? *Policy & Politics*. 32: 3 pp371–86.

Hasenfeld, Y. and Gidron, B. (2005) Understanding Multi-Purpose Hybrid Voluntary Organisations: The Contributions of Theories on Civil Society, Social Movements and Nonprofit Organisations, *Journal of Civil Society*. 1: 2 pp97–112.

Hudson, B. (2004) Analysing Network Partnerships, *Public Management Review*. 6: 1 pp75–94.

Kooiman, J. (2003) *Governing as Governance*, London: Sage.

Kondratowitz, H. J., Tesch-Römer, C. and Motel-Klingebiel, A. (2002) Establishing Systems of Care in Germany: A Long and Winding Road, *Aging – Clinical and Experimental Research*. 14: 4 pp239–46.

Leichsenring, K. (2004) 'Providing Integrated Health and Social Care for Older Persons – a European overview' in K. Leichsenring (ed.) *Providing Integrated Health and Social Care for Older Persons: A European Overview of Issues at Stake*. Aldershot: Ashgate.

Lewis, J. (2002) Older People and the Health-Social Boundage in the UK: Half a Century of Hidden Policy Conflict, *Social Policy & Administration*. 35: 4 pp343–59.

Means, R., Smith, R. and Morbey, H. (2002) *From Community Care to Market Care? The Development of Welfare Services for Older People*, Bristol: Policy Press.

Netten, A., Darton, R., Davey, V., Kendall, J., Knapp, M., Williams, J. F. and Forder, J. (2005) *Understanding Public Services and Care Markets*, London: King's Fund.

Pfau-Effinger, B. (2005) 'Development Paths of Care Arrangements in the Framework of Family Values and Welfare Values' in B. Pfau-Effinger and B. Geissler (eds) *Care Arrangements and Social Integration in European Societies*. Bristol: Policy Press.

Powell, M. and Exworthy, M. (2002) 'Partnerships, Quasi-Networks and Social Policy' in C. Glenndinning, M. Powell and K. Rummery (eds) *Partnerships, New Labour and the Governance of Welfare*. Bristol: Polity Press.

Powell, W. W. (1990) Neither Market nor Hierarchy: Network Forms of Organisation, *Research in Organisational Behaviour*. 12: pp295–336.

Radcliffe, J. and Dent, M. (2005) From New Public Management to the New Governance?, *Policy & Politics*. 33: 4 pp617–22.

Rivard, T. (2006) *Les services d'aide à domicile dans le contexte de l'allocation personnalisée d'autonomie*, Paris: DREES Études et Résultats no. 460.

Roth, G. and Reichert, M. (2004) 'Providing Integrated Health and Social Care for Older Persons in Germany' in K. Leichsenring and A. Alaszewski (eds) *Providing Integrated Health and Social Care for Older Persons: A European Overview of Issues at Stake*. Aldershot: Ashgate.

Taylor, M. (2002) 'Government, the Third Sector and the Contract Culture: UK Experience So Far' in U. Ascoli and C. Ranci (eds) *Dilemmas of the Welfare Mix: The New Structure of Welfare in an Era of Privatization*. New York: Kluwer/Plenum.

Tenbensel, T. (2005) Multiple Modes of Governance: Disentangling the Alternatives to Hierarchies and Markets, *Public Management Review*. 7: 2 pp267–88.

THE EMERGENCE OF LOCAL NON-PROFIT – GOVERNMENT PARTNERSHIPS AND THE ROLE OF INTERMEDIARY ORGANIZATIONS IN JAPAN

Contractual relationships and the limits to co-governance

Ichiro Tsukamoto and Mariko Nishimura

INTRODUCTION: 'PARTNERSHIP', BUT 'CONTRACTUAL RELATIONSHIP'

Since the late 1990s, the non-profit sector has grown rapidly in Japan. The emergence of the sector has been influenced particularly by the rise of public interest in voluntary activities after the Hanshin-Awaji Earthquake of 1995, the enactment of the Law to Promote Specified Non-Profit Activities of 1998 and the expansion of the 'quasi-market' regime facilitating the competition between public and private social service providers since 2000. Reforms of local administration known as 'decentralization' have also resulted in increased interest in non-profit organizations (non-profits) as critical service providers. In addition, as 'government failure' in the delivery of services is increasingly recognized by policymakers and citizens, non-profits are expected to play a major role meeting an 'undersatisfied demand' for public goods (Weisbrod 1975).

In this context, most local governments have been keen to contract their services out to local non-profits. Some local governments have used this to reduce the cost of social services during the fiscal crisis. These government – non-profit contractual relationships are characterized by the 'principal – agent model' and are more market oriented. By contrast, other local governments have engaged in partnerships with local non-profits with the aim of introducing a more community-oriented participatory and democratic type of governance. The latter partnership model is referred to as the 'co-governance model' (Johnson and Osborne 2003; McLaughlin and Osborne 2003; Osborne and McLaughlin 2004), and is occasionally called 'Kyōchi' in Japanese. Under such partnerships, local governments tend to recognize non-profits as inter-dependent and equal partners in dealing with social problems, improving the quality of public services, and encouraging community involvement in local issues.

None the less, most of the partnerships are implemented in the form of contracts, whose frameworks are formed using the top – down approaches of local governments. Non-profits are embedded in such a contractual regime and are more and more reliant on government funding. Furthermore, under this regime, non-profits tend to accept or follow government norms and policies (Smith and Lipsky 1993).

On the other hand, the non-profit sector in Japan has been underdeveloped in creating voluntary and horizontal networks beyond individual organizations. Creating such networks seems to be a critical component of the co-governance-based partnership model. This is because the excessively institutionalized and unilateral relationships dominated by local governments can eventually undermine the independence and autonomy of non-profits. The diversity of non-profits also can be diminished by what sociologists refer to as 'institutional isomorphism' (DiMaggio and Powell 1991). In our hypothesis, an intermediary organization known as an 'infrastructure organization' in the UK and the USA is considered to be indispensable to the equal and mutually dependent partnerships, that is, co-governance model of partnerships.

This work explores the implications of the current emergence of local partnerships between non-profits and local governments and the role of intermediary organizations in Japan. In particular, we focus on the impact of the contractual relationship on organizational change in the non-profits and examine some cases of local intermediary organizations from the perspective of co-governance. Modern governance is commonly characterized in terms of self-organizing, inter-organizational networks (such as 'Compact' and 'LSP' in the UK), and relies on network management (Rhodes 1997). The network covers both state and non-state actors such as non-profits. In this literature, the co-governance concept is related to the co-ordination or management of inter-organizational networks of state and non-state actors. In this governance or network management model, non-profits can be involved in the policy formulation process as well as service delivery.

Non-profits are not only service providers, but also social institutions creating civil society. Van Til (2005) considers the non-profit sector to be a significant institutional contribution to a democratic society. Such a concept is central to our approach to the sector.

CHANGES IN THE WELFARE STATE AND THE EMERGENCE OF THE NON-PROFIT SECTOR IN JAPAN

Since the late 1990s, the social service provision system has dramatically changed in Japan. Due to the implementation of the long-term care insurance system of 2000, a 'quasi-market' or 'welfare mix' regime has been established in the field of elderly care services. Most of the services that municipalities used to deliver have been contracted out to various for-profit and non-profit service providers. According to statistics published by the Ministry of Health, Labour and Welfare in 2004, in the area of domiciliary care services non-profit providers account for 49.8 per cent of the total number of service agencies, businesses for 48.2 per cent and local authorities for just 1.2 per cent.

Administrative reforms, including the transformation of the relationship between central and local governments, have also become a politically critical issue. In April 2000, the Comprehensive Decentralization Law, which stipulates a more equal relationship between central and local governments, came into force. Subsequently, local governments have been required to assume more responsibility for the quality of services and their efficient administration, in accordance with the needs of local residents. The radically ageing population and the stagnant economy in Japan have had an impact on these trends. On the whole, the 'New Public Management' concept has been influential within the statutory sector over the last decade. In this context, local governments have been engaged in outsourcing their existing services and implementing Private Finance Initiatives (PFI).

The new type of non-profit sector has been growing rapidly in Japan, particularly since the late 1990s. The current emergence of the sector was initially caused by rising public interest in the significance of the voluntary activities after the Hanshin-Awaji Earthquake of 1995. Such social change resulted in the enactment of the Law to Promote Specified Non-Profit Activities (the NPO Law) of 1998, as previously mentioned. The law created a new category of incorporated organizations for non-profit and voluntary activities and enabled civic groups to acquire a legal personality known as the 'Specified Non-Profit Corporation' (NPO hōjin) (Pekkanen 2003). NPO hōjin is much easier to incorporate than traditional non-profit corporations because there are fewer government regulations.

Needless to say, our country has a long history of non-profit and community organizations. During the early Meiji Era, traditional non-profit corporations known as 'public interest corporations' were institutionalized with the enactment of the Civil Law of 1897. Public interest corporations known as 'koueki hōjin' are categorized into two types, 'shadan hōjin' (incorporated association) and 'zaidan hōjin' (incorporated foundation). Subsequently, other types of non-profit corporations such as the 'shakai fukushi hōjin' (social welfare corporation), 'gakkō hōjin' (the private school corporation), 'shūkyō hōjin' (religious corporation) and others have been institutionalized, defined and regulated by different laws. The total number of these traditional non-profits is currently estimated to be over 200,000. After incorporation they are, however, strongly regulated and supervised by public authorities with discretionary powers. Thus, civic and grass-roots groups are reluctant to be incorporated into these traditional legal forms.

In terms of statutory frameworks in relation to the promotion of current new types of non-profits, the NPO Law, the long-term care insurance system and a series of local government reforms are quite significant factors. The NPO Law has created not only a new legal framework for the voluntary groups serving the public good, but also new opportunities for their operation in the 'quasi-market' of elderly care services. The service providers under the long-term care insurance system are required to have legal personalities and can then contract with municipalities as accredited service agencies. Municipalities also tend to look for different service providers, including non-profits, in order to contract out their services under the current administrative reforms and fiscal crises. In this context, the non-profit sector in Japan has been regarded as a critical player, especially in the arena of the implementation of public policy.

GROWING PARTNERSHIPS BETWEEN LOCAL GOVERNMENT AND THE NON-PROFIT SECTOR

Non-profits as social institutions are subject to the influence of other institutions that are inter-dependently related to them. In general, the Government is considered the most influential institution for non-profits. Young (2000) argues that government–non-profit relations can be conceptualized as supplementary, complementary or adversarial. In his view, in the supplementary model, non-profits are seen as fulfilling the demand for public goods left undersatisfied by the Government. In the complementary model, non-profits are seen as partners to the Government, helping to carry out the delivery of public goods largely financed by the Government. In the adversarial model, non-profits encourage the Government to make changes in public policy and to maintain accountability to the public.

In Japan, relationships between the Government and non-profits have recently moved towards the complementary model. Since the late 1990s, the relationships have been increasingly embedded in government-led contractual frameworks. None the less, the 'partnership' concept, which is occasionally called 'collaboration', has become a catchword among politicians and government officials. In fact, partnerships with non-profits have been mainly carried out, not at the national, but at the local level. The Japanese national government has not necessarily considered the partnership with non-profits as an effective tool of governance. In addition, the national government has been reluctant to expand tax reliefs, such as tax deduction systems, for the non-profit sector. For this reason, the infrastructure for fostering the sector has been quite poor compared with those in the UK and the USA.

On the other hand, local governments, particularly municipalities, have been keen to promote partnerships with non-profits, spurred on by decentralization and increasing financial difficulties. Local governments have been expected to mobilize and manage local resources (which include non-profits) more effectively and thereby provide local residents with quality services.

Since the late 1990s many local governments have launched into the institutionalization of partnerships with non-profits. However, in most cases, partnership frameworks have been based on contractual relationships, without sufficient infrastructures for the non-profit sector. In fact, according to our national postal survey, 80 percent of responding municipalities are engaged in partnerships with non-profits (Open Research Centre Project 2005). In terms of partnerships in the field of service delivery, around 80 percent of the partnerships are implemented through contractual mechanisms.

Most local government partnership policies are characterized by a lack of strategic perspective. According to our survey, over 55 percent of respondents do not have the basic policies or rules that would be necessary for a systematic promotion of partnerships. Only 14 percent of the respondents have introduced formal performance assessment systems in the partnership, such as the PDCA cycle. Furthermore, most partnerships have been concentrated at the implementation stage of the policy process, the sphere of service delivery, rather than the stage of policy formulation.

The introductory contribution (Brandsen and Pestoff, this issue) makes a distinction between the concepts of co-governance and co-management: co-governance refers to the formulation of the policies in which non-profits participate in the planning of service delivery, whereas co-management refers to the implementation of service delivery. Despite the development of partnerships between local governments and the non-profit sector in Japan, most relationships must be regarded as co-management, without any accompanying co-governance.

In terms of the equality of the relationship, only 38 percent of the respondents consult with individual non-profits when they draw up the document regarding the content of the contract or relationship. Also, 57 percent of the respondents do not provide non-profits with such opportunities, although the consultation and dialogue processes seem to be indispensable to create and preserve trust between both sectors.

In addition, after the revision of the Local Government Law of 2003 many local governments have contracted out the management functions of the public facilities under their ownership such as museums, public halls and sports centres, to non-profits and businesses. Under this revised law, private contractors can receive more discretionary autonomy in their management of the facilities, but the ownership remains in the hands of the local government. Their activities seem to become part of government policy and to be constrained by regulation. Nevertheless, even non-profit intermediary organizations are keen to engage in the management of government facilities for their survival.

In short, most local governments tend to prefer non-profits as service providers from a short-term perspective. As a result, most partnerships have concentrated in the implementation process, in which case there is only co-management without co-governance. Local governments have given less attention to the role of non-profits in building 'trust' or 'social capital' as components of community governance or co-governance. It is clear that most relationships have been dominated and controlled by local governments.

Individual non-profits are keen to contract with local government for fulfilling their financial sustainability, although the contractual relationships are unstable. Consequently they are embedded in competition with other providers, even within the non-profit sector. This trend has been accelerated by contractual relationships in the absence of the co-governance perspective. Accordingly, most relationships between governments and non-profits have been transformed into a principal – agent relationship. Thus, the concept of co-management best describes it.

CHANGES IN THE NATURE OF THE NON-PROFIT SECTOR THROUGH CONTRACTUAL PRINCIPAL – AGENT RELATIONSHIPS WITH GOVERNMENTS

According to the national survey on the Specified Non-Profit Corporations conducted by the Ministry of Economy and Industry (2003; Hamabe and Takahashi 2004), 34.2 percent of the total income of the corporations comes from earned income (excluding government contracts), 18.3 percent from government contracts and grants, 16.8 percent from donations, 11.6 percent from business contracts and grants, 10.8 percent from membership fees and 8.2 percent from other sources. Compared to the results of the previous survey conducted in 2001, government funding as a source of income increased by 7.3 points (from 11.0 percent to 18.3 percent) in just 2 years. The report pointed out that the dependency of non-profits on government funding increased remarkably.

Most government funding is paid in the form of contracts to non-profits. According to the survey on the Specified Non-Profit Corporations in Kanagawa Prefecture (Kanagawa Prefectural Government 2005), 25.5 percent of their total income comes from earned income (excluding government contracts), 20.3 percent from membership fees, 16.4 percent from the long-term care insurance system (contracts with municipalities), 7.6 percent from government contracts, 9.0 percent from donations, 7.9 percent from business contracts and grants, 4.3 percent from government grants and 7.0 percent from other sources. This report showed that most of the government funding was provided for non-profits in the form of contracts.

In this context, non-profits, especially those delivering social services in Japan, have become more and more dependent on government funding. Such non-profits tend to be reliant on the earned income generated from the contract with local government and the quasi-market, such as the long-term care insurance system. Accordingly, the relationship between the Government as a major resource provider and the non-profits has been transformed into a 'principal – agent' relationship.

The distinctive characteristics of non-profits, their independence from government and their diversity seem to be increasingly diminished by the organizational change known as 'institutional isomorphism'. In most cases, non-profits receiving government contracts are required to provide public services under tight government regulations, which are mostly standardized, and the provision of new services needs approval by governments. Accordingly, their diversity and innovative thinking, namely the motivation to develop new ways of responding to needs or develop new services, have diminished. Their behaviour comes to resemble that of the Government.

This development has been started by the contractual relationships regulated by governments. By contrast, the role of the non-profit sector in building trust or horizontal networks of civic engagement, known as 'social capital' or 'relational goods' (Ben-Ner and Gui 2003), has been relatively neglected for many years. Furthermore, current non-profits tend to compete with each other. In recent years, some non-profits have been founded by groups that are largely separated from the social networks of civic engagement. In some cases, local governments promote local citizen groups to establish non-profits in order to contract out their existing services. In this context, the Japanese non-profit sector will become more and more institutionalized and bureaucratic, unless the sector can secure its power as a sector by creating a wider social network beyond individual organizations. Creating such a network is a critical issue for the non-profit sector in its quest for more equal partnerships and more joint planning with governments, which would be typical of co-governance.

THE ROLE OF INTERMEDIARY ORGANIZATIONS IN RELATION TO THE CONTRACTUAL RELATIONSHIP

In Japan, the Government remains the dominant player in complementary relationships (Young 2000). The contractual relationship between both sectors furthers this trend. According to Smith (2005: 375),

> the dilemma of nonprofit managers is that the process of government contracting may undermine a nonprofit's financial stability while encouraging nonprofit organizations to move away from their own distinctive mission and reflect more closely the priorities and goals of government administrators.

Smith (2005: 383) also points out that non-profit management is inextricably connected to political processes such as important political decisions, legislation and administrative rulings. Most non-profits that enter into contract with governments in Japan face a dilemma similar to that described by Smith.

Given that government contracts are part of the political process, non-profits need to enhance their political presence. For this reason, so-called 'intermediary organizations' with an advocacy function on behalf of non-profits are expected to play a significant role in dealing with the dilemma caused by the contracting relationship. These intermediary organizations could be directly involved in the Government's contracting process. Consequently, non-profits could have a collective influence on government policy, including such issues as the rates of contracts, funding levels and contracting procedures. The intermediary organizations may also be helpful in advocating for non-profits in specific disputes between government and individual organizations.

Let us now consider the notion of the intermediary organization. There seems to be no single operational definition. However, the term is generally understood as the following: 'Intermediary organizations play a variety of roles in the non-profit sector, including engaging, convening and supporting critical stakeholders; promoting quality standards and accountability; brokering and leveraging resources; and advocating for effective policies' (Anheier and List 2005: 137).

By this definition, intermediary organizations include support centres, sector-serving organizations, foundations and university-based non-profit research centres. Foundations are the most visible organizations in the USA. Some intermediary organizations are active as national and local umbrella organizations. The intermediary organization is also occasionally called the infrastructure organization. In addition, local development agencies (LDAs) can be categorized as intermediary organizations. LDAs play an important role in providing a framework and infrastructure for voluntary and community action (Osborne 1999).

INTERMEDIARY ORGANIZATIONS IN CONTEMPORARY JAPAN: CASE STUDIES

Since the late 1990s, intermediary organizations known as 'NPO centres' or 'NPO support centres' have been created at the initiative of citizens, in order to support and promote voluntary and non-profit activities at the local and national level. Alongside the emergence of such intermediary organizations, local governments have started to foster non-profit activities and to set up facilities for the specific purpose of supporting non-profits. Such local governmental NPO support facilities or centres are in operation in most of the major municipalities as well as in prefectures around Japan.

More recently, local government NPO support centres have increased rapidly compared to the private non-profit centres incorporated as non-profits. Most governmental support centres were founded by local governments, which then contracted out their management to outside non-profit intermediary organizations. Current administrative reforms have enhanced these trends and resulted in the nation-wide proliferation of governmental support centres. The management of these centres has increasingly been contracted out to outside non-governmental agencies.

In general, Japanese NPO support centres (facilities) can be classified as one of the following three types:

(A) *Government-founded/managed centres*, which are founded, financed and managed by local governments themselves.

(B) *Government-founded/NPO managed centres*, which are founded and financed by local governments and managed by intermediary organizations or other types of non-profits by contract.

(C) *NPO-founded/managed centres*, which are founded and managed by non-profits and operate as pure intermediary organizations.

According to a 2005 analysis of a database on intermediary organizations by the Japan NPO Centre, 151 NPO support centres are in operation in Japan.[2] Of all the centres, 64 centres (42.4 per cent) are owned by local governments but managed by non-profits ('B' type), 48 centres (31.8 per cent) are owned and managed by non-profits ('C' type) and 39 centres (25.8 per cent) are owned and managed by local governments ('A' type).

We will now examine the characteristics of intermediary organizations in Japan based on qualitative case studies, taking into account their classification and the influence of relationships with governments. The case studies were undertaken by the authors during the period 2005–6. The following three organizations are regarded as leading NPO support centres in Japan.

Kanagawa Prefectural Civic Activities Support Centre (category A)

This centre was the first one to be governmentally founded and managed in Japan. It was founded by Kanagawa Prefecture in 1996 and has been financed and managed by the local government.

The centre provides citizen groups and non-profits with information services and facilities such as meeting rooms and lockers. In addition, the centre is engaged in promoting partnerships with non-profits through a unique granting scheme with five-year term financing. The partnership scheme based on the local government grant is called 'Kanagawa Voluntary Fund 21'. Kanagawa Prefectural government makes agreements with non-profits concerning the conditions and rules for partnerships.

The centre does not provide training and consultancy services for non-profits. This is because other NPO support centres founded and managed by non-profits provide such services within the same local community. The centre tries to avoid the duplication of similar services with other private non-profit support centres. Other governmentally founded and managed centres do not necessarily take account of such duplication.

Kyoto Municipal Civic Activities Support Centre (category B)

This support centre is a typical case categorized as a government-founded/NPO-managed centre. Kyoto city founded it and then contracted out the management to the Kyoto NPO Centre in 2003.

The support centre provides information services, consulting, publishing support for brochures and reports via a workroom equipped with computers, printers and other facilities. The latter include workbooths, lockers and mailboxes, training services and co-ordination between activity groups. Kyoto NPO Centre is required to provide users with services stipulated within the contracting framework.

The total income of the Kyoto NPO Centre amounts to 100 million yen (700,000 Euros, £500,000 or US$1 million). Around 70 per cent of its income comes from local government funding in the form of a contract with Kyoto city and only about 30 per cent is generated from the income earned by trading services.

As a result of the contractual framework, Kyoto NPO Centre has been increasingly dependent on government funding. In addition, the decision-making process and rules related to contracted services tend to be tightly controlled by government regulation. According to a chief executive, other local intermediary organizations managing governmental support centres seem to face a similar situation. Under the influence of this contractual relationship, an internal change occurs within the organization. Managers and workers' behaviour becomes more and more bureaucratic, like that of government officials.

Furthermore, the support centre is generally required to provide training services for free under the contractual framework. However, pricing the training or consulting services for other non-profits and charging them seems to be quite important in order to secure income sources for the intermediary organization. Providing training or consulting services for free by the governmental NPO support centre may deprive other intermediary organizations incorporated as non-profits of business chances. In fact, the radical increase in governmental NPO support centres has adversely affected the financial situation of other non-profit intermediary organizations because of unfair competition.

The Kyoto NPO Centre has made efforts to create equal partnerships with Kyoto municipal government regarding the operation of governmental facilities. The 'partnership agreement' between the two parties is the product of these negotiations. The agreement stipulates common rules, including the right of the NPO to consult with the Government regarding the contractual framework and the accountability to citizens. However, this is unusual in Japan.

In terms of governance structure, the Kyoto NPO Centre has a formal structure, such as board meetings and a general assembly, but lacks a representative structure based on membership organizations in the locality.

Community Support Centre Kobe (CS Kobe) (category C)

CS Kobe is categorized as an NPO founded/managed centre. The centre was set up in 1996. It stems from the voluntary group activities struggling with local regeneration after the Hansin-Awaji Earthquake of 1995. The president of this organization, who is also a founding member, learned from the practices of British intermediary organizations.

The mission of the centre is to support and encourage voluntary activities in the local area. Their main areas of work are identifying and meeting local needs, service development, strengthening links between local non-profits and providing support services including information, facilities, consulting and training.

In the fiscal year of 2004, the total income amounted to approximately 100 million yen (700,000 Euros, £500,000 or US$1 million). Around 70 per cent of this total income came from local government funding through project-based contracts, including the management of local facilities. Because of this, the financial structure tends to be unstable and activities are subject to the contractual framework. This is not an exceptional case. Most local intermediary organizations, like CS Kobe and Kyoto NPO Centre, are engaged in managing government facilities for the benefit of their economic survival.

In terms of governance structure, the centre has a formal structure that includes board meetings and a general assembly, but it lacks a representative structure based on membership organizations in the locality.

The key findings of these case studies can be identified as the following (other cases not summarized here are also taken into consideration).

- Intermediary organizations that contract with local governments tend to become financially dependent on government funding and are also subject to political processes dominated by governments.
- Institutional pressures, such as the rules and conditions that are part of the contracting relationship, tend to change internal decision making and behaviour, a process known as 'institutional isomorphism'. Such trends can alienate their functions from advocacy and the exercise of collective influence on government policy on behalf of non-profits.
- Duplication of service delivery occurs between governmental NPO support centres and NPO support centres as private intermediary organizations and undermines the financial sustainability of the intermediary organizations.
- Most intermediary organizations tend to be engaged in the management of governmental facilities in the form of contracts with government for their financial survival.
- The governance structure of the intermediary organizations is not necessarily based on the inter-organizational network of membership organizations. Their representative or networking functions tend to be underdeveloped.

CONCLUSION: THE CHALLENGES OF JAPANESE INTERMEDIARY ORGANIZATIONS IN REALIZING A CO-GOVERNANCE-BASED PARTNERSHIP

Intermediary organizations need to engage with local governments to establish a role for the sector in policy formulation as well as implementation (Osborne and Ross 2001). Intermediary organizations with advocacy and networking functions on behalf of non-profits have some potential capacity to fill the significant role of addressing the dilemma caused by the contractual relationship, that is, the principal–agent model. However, such a role seems to be underdeveloped among Japanese intermediary organizations. Most intermediary organizations are themselves embedded in the government-led contractual relationship and tend to be overly dependent on government funding sources such as contracts, instead of using 'social capital resources' (see later).

In reality, in terms of income sources, the rate of income generated from contracts with governments is approximately 35 per cent in the field of intermediary activities. It is the highest compared with other fields such as community development (25 per cent), environmental protection (24 per cent) and education (23 per cent) according to a 'report of the activities and management of non-profits (the specified non-profit corporation)' conducted by the Ministry of Economy and Industry (Hamabe and Takahashi 2004).

In this institutional environment, which includes the resource dependency on government caused by the contractual relationship, the activities and behaviour of intermediary organizations are likely to be institutionalized and to lose their distinct characteristics and independence from government. The fundraising of non-profits is generally characterized by a mixed resource structure. However, the 'social capital resources' stemming from civil society, namely donations and volunteering (Bode *et al.* 2004: 209) are significantly scarce compared to other countries, such as the UK and the USA. This is closely related to the taxation system in Japan. In this way, Japanese non-profits gain their main resources from 'market' or 'government' mechanisms, not what is called 'social capital'. Non-profits increasingly tend to assume market-oriented or bureaucratic manners. Even intermediary organizations tend to be subject to such conditions. None the less, as we mentioned, they are potentially expected to rely on and actively build 'social capital resources' in Japanese society and create more horizontal social networks within and beyond the non-profit sector. They are also expected to produce 'a sense of identity as a sector' and foster common values beyond individual organizations within the non-profit sector. However, non-profits lack such a sense of identity in the absence of influential intermediary organizations that can build trust or horizontal networks of civic engagement and manage an inter-organizational network of non-profits. Thus, the distinct value of the intermediary activities is not fully recognized by non-profits.

In short, there are two typically Japanese conditions:

(1) Japanese NPOs' main resources are generated from market or government because donations and volunteering are significantly scarce as compared to other countries.
(2) Horizontal social networks within and beyond the non-profit sector and a sense of identity as a sector have not been developed.

Therefore, in the Japanese case, the negative aspects of relationships between governments and non-profits, especially contractual relationships, are very visible. We can therefore draw some lessons for other countries.

(1) Relationships that concern only the implementation of service delivery, especially by contract, can be described as co-management without co-governance.
(2) These relationships are regulated and supervised by governments. Non-profits are required to fulfil the tasks determined by governments. As a result, their characteristics begin to resemble those of government organizations. Their independence from governments, diversity and flexibility seem to be increasingly diminished by the organizational change known as institutional isomorphism.
(3) Individual non-profits, even intermediary organizations, are keen to contract with local governments to preserve their financial sustainability. Consequently, they enter into competition with other providers, even within the non-profit sector.

(4) In order to create equal partnerships with co-governance, the non-profit sector needs to assert its power as a sector by creating a wider social network.

Finally, we briefly identify three key issues for intermediary organizations that could play distinct roles in the co-governance model of partnerships.

(1) *Developing a mixed resource strategy*: this is related to enhancement of their independence from government and greater dependence on social capital resources. Excessive dependence on government funding can result in separating their interests from the voice of citizens and non-profits.
(2) *Establishing representative and networking structures*: this is relevant to strengthening their key function as builders of horizontal networks of civic engagement and of non-profits themselves. In particular, intermediary organizations are required to have real power in co-ordinating and managing the inter-organizational network of non-profits independently from government. The existence of such intermediary organizations is indispensable to co-governance. It can also result in creating a sense of identity as a sector with common values.
(3) *Strengthening political functions such as advocacy and the mobilization of collective influence on government policy*: this focuses on the enhancement of a social infrastructure for the sustainable development of the sector and on changing relationships with governments, including the contract regime. The functions of non-profits can include planning as well as the management of service delivery in collaboration with government. This political function is crucial to the realization of co-governance.

These three challenges are related to each other. Non-profits are not only service providers as agents of governments, but also social institutions rooted in civil society. Therefore intermediary organizations are expected to be embedded in 'civil society', not a 'market-' or 'government'-dominated world.

NOTES

1 In Japan, we generally use 'non-profits' as a broader concept including organized non-profit organizations and more community-based voluntary organizations.
2 http://www.jnpoc.ne.jp/support/index.html.

REFERENCES

Anheier, H. K. and List, R. A. (2005) *A Dictionary of Civil Society, Philanthropy and the Non-Profit Sector*, London: Routledge.

Ben-Ner, A. and Gui, B. (2003) 'The Theory of Nonprofit Organizations Revisited' in H. Anheier and A. Ben-Ner (eds) *The Study of the Nonprofit Enterprise: Theories and Approaches*. New York: Kluwer Academic/Plenum Publishers.

Bode, I., Evers, A. and Schulz, A. (2004) 'A Third Way to Employment and Integration? Social Enterprises in Europe between Workfare and Welfare' in A. Zimmer and C. Stecker (eds) *Strategy Mix for Nonprofit Organisations: Vehicle for Social and Labour Market Integration*. New York: Kluwer Academic/Plenum Publishers.

DiMaggio, P. J. and Powell, W. W. (1991) 'The Iron Cage Revisited: Institutional Isomorphism and Collective Rationality in Organizational Fields' in W. W. Powell and P. J. DiMaggio (eds) *The New Institutionalism in Organizational Analysis*. Chicago, IL: University of Chicago Press.

Hamabe, T. and Takahasi, M. (2004) 'Keizaisyutai Toshiteno NPO' [NPO as Economic Providers] in I. Tsukamoto, S. Furukawa and T. Amemiya (eds) *NPO to Atarashii Shakai Dezain [Non-Profit Organizations and New Social Design]*. Tokyo: Doubunkan.

Johnson, C. and Osborne, S. (2003) Local Strategic Partnerships, Neighbourhood Renewal, and the Limits to Co-governance, *Public Money and Management*. July pp147–54.

Kanagawa Prefectural Government (2005) *Tayouna Hatarakikata Kenkyukai Houkoku [Research Report on the Different Working Styles]*, Yokohama: Kanagawa Prefectural Government.

McLaughlin, K. and Osborne, S. (2003) Modeling the Challenge of Changing Institutional Relationships between Government and the Voluntary Sector in the UK, *Asian Journal of Public Administration*. 25: 1 pp5–30.

Ministry of Economy and Industry (2003) *NPO Hōjin Ankeito Chousa Kekka 2002 [Research Report on the National Survey of the Specified Non-Profit Corporations]*, Tokyo: Ministry of Economy and Industry.

Open Research Centre Project (Meiji University) (2005) *Zenkoku Jichitai Ankeito Chousa Houkokusho: NPO to Jichitai no Kyoudo no Seidoka Jigyouka Sisutemuka ni Kansuru Kenkyu [National Survey on the Institutionalization of the Partnerships between Local Governments and NPOs]*, Tokyo: Meiji University.

Osborne, S. (1999) *Promoting Local Voluntary and Community Action: The Role of Local Development Agencies*, York: Joseph Rowntree Foundation.

Osborne, S. and McLaughlin, K. (2004) The Cross-Cutting Review of the Voluntary Sector: Where Next for Local Government–Voluntary Sector Relationships?, *Regional Studies*. 38: 5 pp573–82.

Osborne, S. and Ross, K. (2001) 'Regeneration: The Role and Impact of Local Development Agencies' in M. Harris and C. Rochester (eds) *Voluntary Organisations and Social Policy in Britain*. New York: Palgrave.

Pekkanen, R. (2003) 'The Politics of Regulating the Non-Profit Sector' in S. P. Osborne (ed.) *The Voluntary and Non-Profit Sector in Japan*. London: Routledge.

Rhodes, R. A. W. (1997) *Understanding Governance: Policy Networks, Governance, Reflexivity and Accountability*, Maidenhead: Open University Press.

Smith, S. R. (2005) 'Managing the Challenges of Government Contracts' in R. D. Herman and Associates (eds) *The Jossey-Bass Handbook of Nonprofit Leadership and Management* (2nd edn). San Francisco, CA: Jossey-Bass.

Smith, S. R. and Lipsky, M. (1993) *Nonprofits for Hire: The Welfare State in the Age of Contracting*, Cambridge: Harvard University Press.

Van Til, J. (2005) 'Nonprofit Organizations and Social Institutions' in R. D. Herman and Associates (eds) *The Jossey-Bass Handbook of Nonprofit Leadership and Management* (2nd edn). San Francisco, CA: Jossey-Bass.

Weisbrod, B. A. (1975) 'Towards a Theory of the Voluntary Non Profit Sector in a Three Sector Economy' in S. P. Edmund (ed.) *Altruism, Morality, and Economic Theory*. New York: Russell Sage.

Young, D. R. (2000) Alternative Models of Government–Nonprofit Sector Relations: Theoretical and International Perspectives, *Nonprofit and Voluntary Sector Quarterly*. 29: 1 pp149–72.

REFLECTIONS ON THE MARKET, NETWORKING AND TRUST

Isabel Vidal

INTRODUCTION

Very frequently research on public administrations and voluntary community organizations (VCOs) overlaps. Research shows the growing importance of the third sector in the different public services in several countries (Salamon 1999). Progressively the analysis focuses on the study of the forms of coordination and cooperation established between the public administrations and third-sector organizations in the governance, management and production of public services. From the 1990s, the existence of this cooperation became evident and some of the forms that this cooperation takes are beginning to be analyzed (Taylor and Hoggett 1994).

To start I refer to three definitions found in the introduction to this collection (Brandsen and Pestoff, this issue) that correspond to three types of coordination. They are the following: (1) *co-production*, understood as citizen involvement in the provision of public services, either individually or through voluntary and community organizations (VCOs), in the provision of the public services as a provider; (2) *co-management*, defined as the collaboration of third-sector organizations and other providers in the provision of public services; and (3) co-governance referring to the role of VCOs in policy formulation and community governance.

Before continuing, two comments on the definitions just mentioned need to be made. The first comment is to express the opinion that activities of co-production as a provider, co-management and co-governance in the domain of public services are not, of course, exclusive to third-sector organizations. Also conventional private organizations have their prominence in the governance, management and provision of public services. The second comment is to indicate that the prominence of VCOs is not homogenous throughout all public services. Rather, its prominence is centered in the community public services, mostly in relational or proximity services (Laville 1992, 1996; Laville and Nyssen 2001) such as social care and social inclusion.

OBJECTIVE

From the definitions given above, the objective here is to provide a reflection from the perspective of economic analysis regarding the why and how of the different forms of governance, management and production of certain public services.

The theoretical approach

From the theoretical approach of *why* the supposition is made that the terms of co-governance, co-management and co-production are associated with the concepts of a division of labor, specialization, networking and collaboration among different players pursuing different goals. The expected objective of this cooperation is a better transmission of information, a better allocation of resources and as a result of this a better adaptation to the preferences of different groups of interest at any given moment.[1] As a consequence of the different players coordinating with one another, there is an exchange of means among them.[2] This implies that each player – the state, a company, VCOs, family or person – depending on the institutional environment in which he/she operates, will develop his/her 'best' plan of action. By plan of action we mean a temporal ordering of limited measures for alternative purposes. The natural operational place is the market in the broad sense and it is identified with the concept of exchange.

The theory of networks and the concept of trust are necessary to explain the *how*. Until the mid-twentieth century, the theory of networks and the concept of trust capital as an important asset in an organization were rarely used by economists (see the large collection of articles on networks found in Grabher and Powell 2004). Research on networks and capital stock was applied to other sectors and players. However, they make it easier for economists interested in third-sector organizations to understand the possibilities of efficiency and economic and financial sustainability of these organizations in an economy with a conventional private sector and a powerful public sector. It is assumed that it is not possible to understand the existence of the organizations of the third sector by their operations alone. The increasing importance of the third sector must be associated with the capacity of its relations, coordination and cooperation with private companies and public administrations.

Analytical basis

In order to provide this reflection, the author uses the knowledge gained during the past four years from two research projects. The first is related to the provision of collective childcare services and the second is found in the domain of social inclusion. These projects are the following:

- Changing Family Structures and Social Policy, concerns the provision of services for young children, the transformation of family, structures and functions, and development in social policy (TSFEPS) in eight European countries.[3]
- The Socio-Economic Performance of Social Enterprises in the field of integration work (PERSE). The project focused on studying the importance of social enterprises in the promotion of public policies supporting people with difficult employability in eleven European member states.[4]

Structure

This reflection is structured as follows: in the second part the appearance of new players in the industry of community services is highlighted. In the third part, as a conclusion, a theoretical reflection is made on the necessary investment that VCOs have to make in trust capital and coordination with the other players in order to be able to attain their current position in the community services industry.

HISTORICAL PERSPECTIVE: DIVERSIFICATION OF USERS, SERVICES PROVIDED AND PLAYERS

From a certain historical perspective, the analysis shows that in the last thirty years, at least, in most of the countries of Western Europe, the users, the types of services provided and also the players operating in the different industries related to community services have diversified.

Family: From producer to producer and community service user

A paradigmatic example is the transformation of the family as a production unit, from being a main producer of family care services to becoming the main user/consumer of care services. According to Netten (2005), the family is the most efficient production unit since it registers the smallest transaction costs. However, what happens with the production capacity of family care services when the main producing member decides to exchange her time resources in the market for a salary? Or, as Netten (2005) indicates, family production can become too complicated, a high number of skills that the family members do not have are needed and then they have to hire or contract care services external to the production unit itself. An important tension of this externalization process of the family care services is the appearance of inefficiencies as a consequence of the appearance of transaction costs (Netten 2005). It is ironical to note the simultaneity between: (a) the reduction in the productive capacity of the family to produce family care services; (b) the progressive increase of the family as buyer/user of care services; and (c) at the same time, the collaboration of the family in the production of such services with the aim of mitigating the inefficiencies generated by the transaction costs, i.e. co-production. (A synthesis of the result of the TSFEPS project may be found in Fraisse 2006.)

New players in the industries of community public services

In Western Europe during the first decades of the second half of the twentieth century, the family's production capacity increased and was complemented with the construction of a new public production capacity. However, it is theoretically and practically impossible to organize such a complex process of specialization and exchange in a centralized way. Thus, the increasing provision of a more and more diversified offer of services and users of welfare goods has made it inevitable for the public administration itself to resort to private organizations, primarily due to their smaller size and their specialization. The result is the presence of new players coming from the private sector, both lucrative and nonlucrative or for-profit and nonprofit, in the whole process of management, elaboration and provision of these public services.

Let us shift our focus to the organizations of the nonprofit sector. They have always existed, so why then the recent interest among scholars in social sciences? One possible answer may be because of the increasing prominence of the organizations of the third sector in the industry of welfare goods. This strong prominence is modifying the traditional *modus operandi* of some VCOs. The development of the welfare goods market is enabling the growth of business for a certain profile of organizations in the third sector: the so-called social enterprises (Borzaga and Defourny 2004; Nyssen 2006). Nonprofit organizations serve the community and multistakeholders; but, they are also professionalizing their management, increasing their productive capacities and more and more becoming oriented to the public and/or private market. This business professionalization of the VCOs enables them, together with the conventional public and private sectors, to develop partnership activities in areas where the solitary operation of public administrations has proven disappointing: e.g. social inclusion into work of people with difficult employability.

The PERSE Project underlines the need for networking among the different players who for different reasons may be interested in being included in the market of people with difficult employability. They coordinate and cooperate with each other, hoping that this cooperation will result in benefits for all the partners in the network. (Consult the EMES web page: www.emes.net, where eleven national reports analyze the importance of social enterprises for inclusion of people with difficult employability in the job market.) The PERSE Project also provides examples of co-governance between territorial administrations and social enterprises in the design of concrete laws and policies that make easier the inclusion of people with difficult employability in the job market. VCOs, as a provider of social inclusion public services, demonstrate good co-management practices among VCOs, conventional companies and territorial public administrations. This promotes the economic and financial sustainability of the social enterprises for insertion and provides examples of co-production. Currently, it is perhaps in the sector of social inclusion where more networking and trust relations are being developed among the different interested parties, allowing the use of an expression coined by McLaughlin (2004), local global compact.

CONCLUSIONS: NETWORKING AND TRUST

As Brandsen and van Hout (this issue) noted earlier, what is most surprising is not only the spectacular increase of private providers, but rather how these providers are interacting with the responsible public administrations and with families through different forms of networking. An efficient operation of the group of players working in a network includes ingredients such as credibility, reputation and mutual trust. This is necessary since it is impossible to foresee all the contingencies that may affect their relations in the future. This is a consequence of a risk of the surge of opportunistic behavior and the importance of the 'ideology' or of the 'motivation' among the different players taking part in the network.

For an organization taking part in the network, it means that its network partners and other organizations value the organization positively and think that it does things properly. Therefore, it can be deduced that the other network partners trust the organization. Thus, trust must be considered an important asset and part of the organization's capital. More precisely, it is the core of the social capital stock accumulated by the organizations among their partners and/or interest groups.

However, social capital and trust capital are two concepts to which economists have paid little attention until now. To start paying attention to and to value the concept of social capital stock, economists must modify their traditional analysis. Economic theory too frequently analyzes the organization – private or public – from the perspective of an individual player. The concepts of co-governance, co-management and co-production require us to go from this individual analysis to another type of analysis incorporating the mutual influence of the different players collaborating with one another and the reciprocal relations between them. It also requires that we consider the effect of uncertainty in economic decisions and social relations, as well as the effect of an information asymmetry among the different players cooperating with one another (Pérez 2005).

In the context of networking for the financing, production and provision of welfare goods, what do we mean by social capital? One answer is the generation of trust and cooperation relations and their value as an intangible asset (Williamson 1993). The trust in a certain organization by some of the other players may be defined as the total time that the groups of interest do *not* have to spend verifying their activities. The strong development and importance of VCOs in the provision of local public services shows the trust that public administrations place in VCOs. To gain this trust, VCOs had to professionalize, become more transparent and gain the support of the families. Thus, VCOs have previously carried out a process of accumulation of trust capital in order to become an important partner of territorial public administrations in the design of new public policies, in the management of these public policies and in the final phase of co-production. If there is trust in the work carried out by the VCOs this means that public administrations think that the relations with the VCOs are going to result in potential profits for both parties.

NOTES

1 We are using an evolutionary approach, where demands and offers evolve constantly.

2 The means can be goods, services or information. The money exchange is one type of exchange. The payment of taxes in exchange for receiving public services is another kind of exchange. In this reflection the market will be identified with a larger concept of exchange.

3 Belgium, Bulgaria, France, Germany, Italy, Spain, Sweden, the UK. The national TSFEPS reports are available on the EMES site: www.emes.net.

4 Germany, Belgium, Denmark, Spain, Finland, France, Ireland, Italy, Portugal, Sweden and the UK. An outcome of this research work is found in Nyssen (2006).

REFERENCES

Borzaga, C. and Defourny, J. eds (2004) *The Emergence of Social Enterprise,* Routledge Studies in the Management of Voluntary and Non-Profit Organizations, London & New York: Routledge.

Fraisse, L. (2006) The Third Sector in the Local Governance of Childcare Services, *Cies.* 39. Available at www.grupcies.com.

Grabher, G. and Powell, W. (2004) *Networks* (two vols), Critical Studies in Economic Institutions No. 6, Cheltenham, UK: Edward Elgar.

Laville, J. L. (1992) *Les Services de Proximité en Europe: Pour une Economie Solidaire*, Paris: Syros.

—— (1996) 'Los Servicios de Proximidad: Una Elección de la Sociedad' in I. Vidal (ed.) *Inserción Social por el Trabajo: Una Visión Internacional*. Barcelona: Cies.

Laville, J. L. and Nyssen, M. eds (2001) *Les Services Sociaux entre Associations, État et Marché: L'Aide aux Personnes Âgées*, Paris: La Decouverte.

McLaughlin, K. (2004) Towards a 'Modernized' Voluntary and Community Sector? Emerging Lessons from Government – Voluntary and Community Sector Relationships in the UK, *Public Management Review*. 6: 4 pp555–62.

Netten, A. (2005) 'The Social Production of Welfare' in M. Knapp, D. Challis, J.-L. Fernández and A. Netten (eds) *Long-Term Care: Matching Resources and Needs*. Aldershot, Brookfield, NJ & Singapore: Ashgate.

Nyssen, M. ed. (2006) *Social Enterprise: At the Crossroads of Market, Public Policies and Civil Society*, London & New York: Routledge.

Pérez, F. ed. (2005) *La Medición del Capital Social: Una Aproximación Económica*, Madrid: Fundación BBVA.

Salamon, L. ed. (1999) *Global Civil Society: Dimensions of the Nonprofit Sector*, Baltimore, MD: Johns Hopkins, Center for Civil Society Studies.

Taylor, M. and Hoggett, P. (1994) Trusting in Networks? The Third Sector and Welfare Change, in Perri 6 and I. Vidal (eds) *Delivering Welfare: Repositioning Non-Profit and Co-operative Action in Western European Welfare States*. Barcelona, Cies.

Williamson, O. (1993) Calculativeness, Trust and Economic Organization, *Journal of Law and Economics*. 34: 453–502. Cited en Pérez Garcia, F. ed. (2005) *La Medición del Capital Social: Una Aproximación Económica*, Madrid: Fundación BBVA.

PATTERNS OF CO-PRODUCTION IN PUBLIC SERVICES

Some concluding thoughts

Victor Pestoff, Stephen P. Osborne and Taco Brandsen

INTRODUCTION

In recent years, there has been a growing body of literature on the reform of European economies and systems of social protection. Much of this literature deals with changes (or lack of them) in labor markets. However, it fails to take account of the significant potential contribution to economic innovation through the provision of public services. One method for introducing more innovation in this area has been to involve different types of actors in service provision, including third-sector organizations.

In many European countries, public service provision has never been equated with state provision. Voluntary and non-profit organizations traditionally played a major role in providing public services, especially in Continental countries. In the European Union generally, the significance of such organizations in the public domain has increased over recent decades. As a consequence, systems of provision increasingly combine different mechanisms of co-ordination and different types of actors (elsewhere termed 'the welfare mix', see Brandsen *et al.* 2005; Evers 2005). There have also been various ways in which users have been involved in service provision, as co-producers of the services they receive. Such arrangements are believed to contribute both to innovation and commitment in the public services.

Research into these various types of arrangements has so far been scattered, focusing on either governance issues or on production, on volunteers or professionals, on organizations or individuals. However, there is much to learn from drawing the different manifestations of the third sector's role together, as they each represent an element of the third sector within the public services, expressed in different ways. An interesting question for research and practice is how different combinations of such elements are and should be embedded, given the variations in national structures of service provision. The collection of studies presented here offers a stepping-stone in progressing towards an answer. In this concluding contribution, we attempt to draw some lessons from them that could inform the future research agenda.

THE CONCEPTS OF CO-PRODUCTION, CO-MANAGEMENT AND CO-GOVERNANCE

In the introduction, we attempted to distinguish between three different roles of the third sector in relation to public services:

- *Co-governance* refers to an arrangement, in which the third sector participates in the planning and delivery of public services.
- *Co-management* refers to an arrangement, in which the third sector produces services in collaboration with the state.
- *Co-production*, in our more restricted use of the term, refers to an arrangement where citizens produce their own services at least in part. The latter could also

refer to autonomous service delivery by citizens without direct state involvement, but with public financing and regulation.

These concepts were partly traced back to the debate on user involvement. The concept of co-production was initially developed in America in the late 1960s to describe and delimit the involvement of ordinary citizens in the production of public services. It had a clear focus on the role of individuals or groups of citizens in the production of such services, although their involvement also had clear ramifications for both the meso and macro levels of society. More recently, it has been given a normative angle. Co-production, according to some proponents, could play a significant role in the renewal of democratic political systems and the welfare state (Pestoff 2007, forthcoming).

There have also been efforts to expand the meaning of the concept. In the UK, co-production has been used to analyse the role of voluntary and community organizations (VCOs) in the provision of public services (Osborne and McLaughlin 2004). Our threefold distinction builds on their work and attempts to bring together related, but different perspectives on the role of the third sector. However, by no means do we regard this typology as the last word on this issue. Rather, we prefer to view it as the starting point for what will hopefully be a long and fruitful debate.

We will now set out some potential avenues for future discussion, based on points made in this collection of studies. They concern, respectively, the relationships between different roles of the third sector, links with the analysis of welfare state reform and the function of co-production.

THE RELATIONSHIPS BETWEEN DIFFERENT ROLES OF THE THIRD SECTOR

One benefit of our approach is that it encourages a more comprehensive view of the different roles the third sector may have within a complex structure of service provision. Future research could explore the nature of these relationships more systematically. For example, a number of authors in this collection observe a trade-off between co-management and co-governance. It would certainly be interesting, not least for the third sector itself, to know whether this is a systematic trade-off or merely a temporary phenomenon. Also, there may be an advantage in a perspective on third-sector roles that embraces all its potential manifestations. For instance, the discussion of childcare and eldercare points to the need for a closer look at the unique nature of services, which often imply the active participation of clients or their relatives. The concept of co-production in providing public services might have put a somewhat different angle to Bode's interesting comparison of three European countries.

It is also useful to re-evaluate the third sector's influence on public services across the entire policy cycle and not simply to restrict it to influence on policymaking through advocacy. The output side of the political system (Easton 1965) deserves closer attention in both democratic and welfare theory. Opportunities for influencing the actual services may be much greater further down the cycle (thereby linking the third sector to the field of implementation studies). The observations of Brandsen and van Hout in this collection show that, even if the role of organizations is restricted to co-management, there may still be scope for significantly influencing the final result, to an extent that goes beyond 'fine-tuning'. A problem is, perhaps, that researchers have started to believe in the top–down, principal–agent perspective that is espoused by many governments, when in fact there is considerable autonomy for the agents if they take advantage of strategic opportunities.

LINKING THE THIRD SECTOR TO THE ANALYSIS OF WELFARE STATE REFORM

Given that the services delivered by third-sector organizations are mostly of a social nature, it seems logical to link it more closely to the debate on welfare state reform. Over the past decade, the latter has been strongly influenced by the notion of typologies of welfare states (cf. Titmuss 1974; Esping-Andersen 1990). These certainly offer opportunities for cross-national analysis. For instance, Prentice's contribution explicitly links the Canadian experience to the liberal welfare regime type, in which childcare is primarily delivered through markets. This invites comparison; would third-sector services and co-production place as many burdens on women as active parents in a more 'family-friendly' society of the Scandinavian type? Turning to the elderly, in Bode's analysis of Germany, France and England, we find countries representing two of Esping-Andersen's three 'regimes', the continental conservative or corporatist and the liberal regime types. Do these theoretical regime differences have any bearing for the role of third-sector organizations in the provision of eldercare?

However, the studies in this collection also give cause to be wary of using the regime typology for an analysis of the third-sector's role. Not only has the third sector been left out of mainstream regime typologies, but research on regimes has also tended to focus on formal arrangements (mostly concerning income transfer rather than service provision) at the national level. This ignores the local level, where many government–third-sector partnerships appear to have been realized regardless of the type of regime. Also, it has bypassed the issue of quality. The latter is more significant for services than for income transfer and is an issue where the third sector's distinctive characteristics are more likely to be relevant.

THE FUNCTION OF CO-PRODUCTION

Finally, there is the question what co-production does, or in other words, what its actual function is. How exactly is the third sector related to governments, in terms of service delivery? Is it supplemental, complementary, alternative or perhaps even adversarial? To take the case of childcare: is third-sector childcare primarily a supplement to public childcare, perhaps one that prevents or hinders governments from developing a universal early learning and childcare programme, since other services are already available? Or, is the third sector perhaps a complement to the public sector, one that can help to develop it in tandem by providing some best practice examples of high-quality care that may be emulated by public providers and/or demanded by parents elsewhere?

Future research could help to conceptualize the different types of functions more systematically and assess them on a cross-sectoral and/or cross-national basis. In the countries examined in this collection, the function of the third sector appears to be either supplementary or complementary. It would be especially interesting to include developing countries in an international sample, where there is more chance of the third sector having an alternative or adversarial function. This might help to determine with more precision which roles and functions of the third sector are more likely or more appropriate under certain conditions.

REFERENCES

Brandsen, T., Van de Donk, W. and Putters, K. (2005) Griffins or Chameleons? Hybridity as a Permanent and Inevitable Characteristic of the Third Sector, *International Journal of Public Administration*. 28: 9–10 pp749–65.

Easton, D. (1965) *A Systems Analysis of Political Life*, New York: J. Wiley & Sons.

Esping-Andersen, G. (1990) *The Three Worlds of Welfare Capitalism*, Cambridge: Polity Press.

Evers, A. (2005) Mixed Welfare Systems and Hybrid Organizations: Changes in the Governance and Provision of Social Services, *International Journal of Public Administration*. 28: 9–10 pp737–48.

Osborne, S. and McLaughlin, K. (2004) The Cross-Cutting Review of the Voluntary Sector: Where Next for Local Government Voluntary Sector Relationships?, *Regional Studies*. 38: 5 pp573–82.

Pestoff, V. (2007) *The Redemocratization of the Welfare State* (forthcoming).

Titmuss, R. M. (1974) *Social Policy: An Introduction*, London: George Allen & Unwin.

NOTES ON CONTRIBUTORS

Ingo Bode is researcher and lecturer associated to the Institute of Sociology at the University of Duisburg-Essen (Germany) where he specializes in organization studies, political sociology and the comparison of welfare systems. He has published international articles on the voluntary sector and social administrations and is author of *The Culture of Welfare Markets: The International Recasting of Pension and Care Systems* (Routledge, forthcoming in 2007).

Taco Brandsen is Associate Professor at the Nijmegan School of Management, Nijmegan University, the Netherlands. He specializes in public policy, organizational analysis and welfare state reform. His current research focuses on the governance and management of mixed systems of service provision.

Mariko Nishimura is Professor of Public Policy at Meijigakuin University, in Tokyo, Japan, where she specializes in health and elderly care, the non-profit sector and public policy. She is the co-author of *NPO and New Social Design* (2004). Current projects include comparative studies on relationships between non-profits and governments in Japan, the UK and the USA.

Stephen P. Osborne is Professor of International Public Management in the School of Management and Economics at the University of Edinburgh. He is Editor-in-Chief of *Public Management Review* and Founding Chair of the International Research Society for Public Management.

Victor Pestoff is Professor of Political Science, Mid-Sweden University, Östersund and also affiliated with Ersta Sköndal College, Stockholm, Sweden. He specializes in social economy, the third sector and the democratization of the welfare state. He is author of *Beyond the Market and State* (1998) and *A Democratic Architecture for the Welfare State* (2007).

Susan Prentice is Associate Professor of Sociology at the University of Manitoba, where she specializes in childcare, social movements and public policy. Her most recent book is *Changing Child Care: Five Decades of Advocacy and Policy in Canada* (2001). Current projects include social and economic impact studies of childcare in Manitoba and a review of privatization and commercialization of childcare in Canada, Australia and the UK.

Ichiro Tsukamoto is Professor of Public Management at the School of Business Administration, Meiji University, in Tokyo, Japan, where he specializes in non-profit management, social enterprise and corporate social responsibilities. He is the editor of *NPO and New Social Design* (2004) and *CSR Over the Border* (2006) (Japanese version only).

Eelco van Hout is researcher and lecturer at the Tilburg School of Politics and Public Administration and Tias Business School of Tilburg University. He specializes in organizational change, organization management in third-sector organizations with a special interest in elder care and higher education. His current research projects include several parallel studies of (change) management and performance management of hybrid elder care and higher education organizations in the Netherlands.

Isabel Vidal is Professor of Economics at the University of Barcelona and she is a researcher at the Research Centre in Economics and Society (CIES). She specializes in social economy, the third sector, social enterprise and corporate social responsibility. Her current research focus is on governance and networking. She has published international articles on social economy and social enterprise. She is co-author, together with Jordi Morros, of *Responsabilidad Social Corporativa* (2005).

Index

accountability 34, 39, 48–50, 54, 56, 65, 79, 82
ad-sourcing 54
administration 49, 54, 66, 71, 76–7, 82–3, 95
adversarial model 79, 102–3
advocacy 8, 41, 82, 86, 88, 101
affluence 37–8
aide ménageaire 65
Alford, J. 17–18
alliances 65, 67, 70
altruism 38–40
America 3, 12
ancillary activities 15, 22
assessment procedures 69
associational alliances 67
asymmetric dependence 48–9
audit society 50
auspices 34, 36
Australia 17
autonomy 48–9, 51, 64, 76, 80, 101–2

banks 67
Barber, B. 12, 24
Belgium 14, 19–20
benchmarks 68
benefit schemes 66
boards of directors 31–2, 38, 40
Bode, I. 7, 59–74, 101–2
bottom-up services 33, 49
boundaryless organizations 48
Brandsen, T. 1–9, 31, 45–57, 79, 95, 99–103
Brazil 16
Britain *see* United Kingdom
Bulgaria 14, 19, 22
bureaucracies 61
business culture 70
buyer-beware market 36

Caledon Institute 38
Canada 6, 29–41, 102
care centres 64
case sensitivity 62
cash options 64
centralization 3, 16
Changing Family Structures and Social Policy 14, 19, 93
Child Care Expense Deduction 35
childcare 4, 6, 11–25, 29–41, 93, 101–3
Christmas 21
citizenship 12–25
civic orientations 61–2, 70
Civil Law 78
civil servants 12
civil society 2, 6, 12–13, 25, 77, 87–8
class 39
Cleveland, G. 35–6
clientelism 71
clients 4, 16–17, 39, 50–3, 101
co-governance 4–8, 23–4, 31
  concept 100–1
  limits 75–88
  networks 59–71
  theory 92–3, 95–6
  trade-offs 101
co-management 4–8, 21, 23, 31
  concept 100–1

limits 79–80, 87
networks 45–56
theory 92–3, 95–6
third sector 34
trade-offs 101–2
co-operation 24, 46, 49–52
networks 55–6, 62, 65–9
theory 92–3, 95–6
co-operatives 20–3, 25, 32
co-ordination 4, 7, 33–4, 50
limits 88
networks 55, 61, 65, 67–8, 70–1, 77
patterns 100
theory 92–5
co-production 3–5, 52, 71
childcare 22–5, 29–41
concept 100–1
effects 45–56
function 102–3
introduction 1–8
models 14–19
patterns 99–103
reform 102
theory 92–3
trade-offs 101
co-sourcing 54
Cole, A. 71
commercial sector 35–6, 40–1
Community Care Act 68
Community Support Centre Kobe (CS Kobe) 85–6
community-based organizations 33, 38
competition 49–50, 52, 55–6
networks 60–2, 65, 67, 69
relationships 76, 80, 85, 87
competitive advantage 50, 65
complementary model 79, 102
complexity 52, 56
Comprehensive Decentralization Law 77
conservatives 32, 35, 38, 102
contracts 23, 47, 54–6, 60, 68, 75–88, 94
core tasks 47, 50–1
corporate identity 68
corporations 36, 78, 80
corporatism 4, 7, 20–1, 60, 63, 66, 70–1, 102
cost/benefit analysis 16
Coventry University 56
creches 30
crime 15
cultural traditions 60
customer focus 17

Davies, J.S. 62
daycare 30
decentralization 76, 79
Dekker, P. 3
democracy 6, 12–14, 18–19, 21–5, 39, 71, 76–7, 101
developing countries 16, 103
differentiation 46–9, 51, 53, 56
diplomas 66
diversification 50–1, 53, 55–6, 94–5
division of labour 8, 14, 20, 23, 47, 63, 92
domain consensus 62–4, 66, 68–71
domiciliary care 59–71, 77
dual systems 67
duplication 84
Dutch *see* Netherlands

Early Childhood Development 30, 34
early excellence centres (EECs) 20
economics 8, 14, 19, 22, 24
co-management 50
networks 61–3, 68–9
reform 100
relationships 77, 85
theory 93, 95–6
third sector 31, 36
trust 92
economies of scale 65
EGPA 2

eldercare 7, 17–18, 25, 39
co-governance 59–71
co-management 46–7, 52, 54, 56
limits 77–8
patterns 101
elections 12, 21
EMES 95
employment 66–7
England 7, 14, 19–20, 60, 67–71, 102
entrepreneurs 41, 64
Esping-Anderson, G. 102
ethics 61
Europe 4, 6–7, 11–25, 52, 60, 93–4, 100–1
European Union (EU) 20, 100
external relations 49–50

faith-based agencies 64
family role 94–6, 102
federalism 33
feedback 14
fees 19, 30–2, 36–7, 40, 68, 81
festivals 21
Finance Canada 35
fiscal crisis 76
for-profit organizations *see* profit
France 7, 14, 19–20, 22–4
eldercare 60, 63, 65–7, 69–71
patterns 102
free-riders 16
frustrated policy capacity 33–5, 40
funding 6–7, 13, 19, 22
co-management 47, 50–2, 54
contracts 76, 81–2, 84–8
networks 64, 66, 68–9
third sector 30–2, 34–6, 40–1

Galbraith, J.K. 13
gatekeepers 55, 64–5, 67–8
gender 38–40
geographic inequity 37–8
Germany 2–3, 7, 14, 19–20
eldercare 60, 63–5, 69–70
reform 22–4, 102
globalization 17
good society 25
government role *see* state role
grants 84
grassroots groups 78

Hanshin-Awaji Earthquake 76, 78, 85
Harvey, D. 37
hierarchy 55, 60–1, 68–9, 71
high-income users 66–7
Hirst, P. 6, 13, 24–5
horizontal co-operation 67–8
horizontal networks 76, 87
hospitals 65, 68
housekeeping 63
Housing Association Diversification in Europe 46
Hudson, B. 60
hybridization 48–9, 52, 61

ideology 2, 71, 96
implementation 102
in-kind contributions 19–20
in-sourcing 54
incorporation 78, 83
Independent Living movement 25
Indiana University 3
information asymmetry 96
infrastructure 34, 63, 65–8, 71, 76, 79, 88
initiatives 20–3
inner-city areas 37
innovation 50–1, 56, 60, 81, 100
institutions 14–15, 21, 24
contracts 76–9, 81, 86–7, 93
networks 63, 65, 70
insurance 64–7, 77–8, 81
integration 46–9, 51–4, 56
intermediary organizations 75–88
interventionism 71

interviews 46, 63
invisible hand 37
Ireland 46, 56
IRSPM 2
isomorphism 76, 81, 86–7
Italy 14, 19, 46, 56

Japan 7, 25, 75–88
Jones, G. 71

Kanagawa Prefectural Civic Activities Support Centre 84
Krashinsky, M. 35–6
Kyoto Municipal Civic Activities Support Centre 84–5

Law to Promote Specified Non-Profit Activities (NPO Law) 76, 78
leadership 33
leaking 51
legislation 33, 36
liberals 30–3, 60, 71, 102
Lipsky, M. 32
lobbying 65, 69–70
Local Authorities 67–8, 77
Local Care Networks 46
local corporatism 66
local development agencies (LDAs) 82
local global compact 95
Local Government Law 80
Local Strategic Partnerships 4, 68–9
low-income users 31–2, 37–8, 66, 68

McLaughlin, K. 5, 95
management style 46, 52, 56
Managing Hybrid Care Services 46
marginalization 38
market orientation 76, 87
market rationale 12, 66, 68–9, 71
marketing 62, 67
marketization 60, 62–3, 65, 69–70
Martin, P. 32
media 40
Meiji Era 78
Ministry of Economy and Industry 80
Ministry of Health, Labour and Welfare 77
missionary organizations 55–6
Montessori approach 25
motherhood mandate 39–40
Multilateral Framework Agreement on Early Learning and Care 30

National Health Service (NHS) 67–8
neo-liberals 12
nervous network governance 71
Netherlands 2–3, 46, 52, 56
Netten, A. 94
networks 3, 6–8, 95–6
  changing 69–71
  co-governance 59–71
  co-management 45–56
  Japan 76–7, 81, 86–8
  management model 77
  parents 21
  relations 65, 67–8
  theory 92
  trust 91–7
New Public Management (NPM) 2, 18, 60, 71, 77
Nigeria 16
Nishimura, M. 7, 75–89
non-profit sector 2–3, 7, 23
  childcare 33–8, 41
  limits 75–88
  networks 59–71, 95
  role 100
nurseries 30, 37
nursing 63, 66–8

one desk policies 51
Organization for Economic Co-operation and Development (OECD) 30, 35
organizational theory 46–7, 50–6, 102

Osborne, S. 5, 8, 99–103
Ostrom, E. 16, 22
out-patients 63
outsourcing 2, 49, 54, 77

parallel production 15, 23
paramedics 65
parent associations 20, 22–3
parents 6, 13, 17–21, 23–5, 30–2, 37–41, 102–3
participatory model 18–22
parties 21
partnerships 75–88
PDCA cycle 79
pedagogy 19–20, 22–5, 32
Percy, S. 15–16
performance management 2
PERSE 93, 95
persuasion 55
Pestoff, V. 1–9, 11–27, 31, 79, 99–103
Peters, G. 18
philanthropy 30
politics 14, 16, 18–20, 22
  Canada 30, 33, 40–1
  childcare 24
  co-management 46, 51, 53
  Japan 77, 79, 82, 86, 88
  patterns 101
polycentrism 16
post-corporatism 70
poverty 38
pre-school services 19, 23, 36
Prentice, S. 6, 29–44, 102
principal-agent model 76, 80–1, 86, 102
Private Finance Initiatives (PFI) 77
private provision 64
private sector 3, 6, 13, 17
  childcare 25, 33–4, 36–8, 41
  networks 66
  trust 93, 95
privatization 2, 12, 32–3, 35–8
process management 48
procurement 50
professional associations 63–4
professionalism 61, 64, 66–7, 70–1, 95–6
profit 2, 7, 21–3, 25, 30–1, 35–6, 59–71, 95
public goods 47
public interest corporations 78
public sector 6, 13, 17–18
  childcare 23, 25, 30, 33
  eldercare 62, 67, 69
  reform 103
  trust 93, 95
public service delivery 1–8, 47–9, 51, 53–4, 60

quality issues 35–6, 65, 68, 70–1, 76–7, 82, 102–3
quangos 69
quasi-markets 7, 47, 53, 55
  eldercare 60, 64, 68, 70–1
  limits 76–8, 81

race 39
rationalization 46–7, 52
reciprocity 62, 96
referenda 19
regulation 25, 31, 34, 36
  childcare 39–40
  co-management 47, 50
  eldercare 60, 64–7, 69–71
  Japan 78, 80–1, 84
relationality 53–4, 81
residential services 68
resource dependency theory 51
responsibilities 51
rewards 17
rhetoric 46
Rich, R.C. 15–16
Rosenau, V. 36
Rosentraub, M. 15
Royal Commission on the Status of

Women 33
rural areas 37

sanctions 17
Scandinavia 12, 17–18, 102
self-help groups 25
service shops 67
Sharp, E.B. 14
single parents 20
skills 46–7, 52–3, 55–6
skimping 35
Smith, S.R. 32, 82
social capital 37–8
social corporatism 63
Social Service Departments 68
Social Union Framework Agreement (SUFA) 33
socialism 19
Socialstationen 64
Socio-Economic Performance of Social Enterprises 93
solidarity 17
sourcing 53–4
Spain 14, 19
special needs 36
specialization 8, 15, 92, 94
Specified Non-Profit Corporations 78, 80–1
staff/child ratios 35–6
staffing 46–7, 52–4, 56
stakeholders 19, 21, 24–5, 46
co-management 55
contracts 82
networks 67, 69
trust 95
state role 2–3, 5–6, 12
Canada 31, 37
childcare 18–19, 25
concepts 101
eldercare 60, 63, 65, 71
Japan 75–88
networks 46–7, 49, 51–2
reform 100
structure 46–7, 50, 52, 54–5, 85, 93–4, 100
subsidies 31–2, 34, 36–7, 63, 65
suburban areas 37
SUFA 34
supervision 65
support centres 83–7
Sweden 3, 14, 18–24
synergies 4, 23

task demarcation 49–51
taxation 12, 17–18, 35, 38, 68, 79, 87
Taylorism 64
technology 14
third sector 1–8, 12, 23–5, 38
childcare 29–41
co-management 46–9, 51, 53–4, 56
eldercare 60–1, 63, 69–71
involvement 100
relationships 101–2
theory 93
trust 92, 95
Throne Speech 30, 41
Tilburg University 56
time crunch 38–40
top-down approach 21, 51, 76, 102
transaction costs 94
Truelove, Marie 37
trust 8, 55–6, 80–1, 91–7
TSFEPS Project 14, 19, 21, 93–4
Tsukamoto, I. 7, 75–89

undersatisfied demand 76
United Kingdom (UK) 2–4, 46, 56
contracts 76–7, 79, 85, 87
eldercare 63, 71
reform 101
United States (US) 4, 16, 23, 76, 79, 82, 101
unskilled staff 66, 68
urban centres 37

Van Hout, E. 6, 45–57, 95, 102
Van Til, J. 77
vertical co-operation 67–8
Vidal, I. 8, 91–7
voluntary community organizations (VCOs) 4, 92–6, 101
voluntary sector 2, 12–13
  childcare 16, 18, 30, 32, 39–41
  eldercare 62–3, 65–71
  organizations 46, 61, 67, 70
  role 100–1
Voluntary Sector Compact 4
volunteers 39–40, 64–6, 68, 70, 87, 100
vouchers 18–19, 64, 66, 70

Waldorf approach 25
Walzer, M. 6, 12–13, 24–5
Warren, R. 15
web pages 95
welfare
  associations 63
  bureaucracies 61–2, 69–70
  capitalism 60
  goods 95–6
  mix 77, 100
  professionalism 61–3, 68–70
  theory 101
welfare state 2, 6–8, 12–14
  childcare 18, 22, 24–5, 30, 41
  co-management 46, 49, 56
  Japan 77–8
  reform 101–2
Wohlfahrtsverbände 63
Workshop in Political Theory and Policy Analysis 3
World War II 63

You Bet I Care! 35
Young, D.R. 79
youth activities 17

zero-sum game 24